T0301980

Customer Needs and Strategic Management

Left-Right Circles Analysis

Customer Needs and Strategic Management

Left-Right Circles Analysis

Andrew Chi-fai Chan

The Chinese University of Hong Kong, Hong Kong

Joseph H L Ko

Yau Lee Holdings Limited, Hong Kong

Conrad Wong

Yau Lee Holdings Limited, Hong Kong

Diamond Tai

The Chinese University of Hong Kong, Shenzhen, China

World Scientific

NEW JERSEY · LONDON · SINGAPORE · BEIJING · SHANGHAI · HONG KONG · TAIPEI · CHENNAI · TOKYO

Published by

World Scientific Publishing Co. Pte. Ltd.

5 Toh Tuck Link, Singapore 596224

USA office: 27 Warren Street, Suite 401-402, Hackensack, NJ 07601

UK office: 57 Shelton Street, Covent Garden, London WC2H 9HE

Library of Congress Cataloging-in-Publication Data

Names: Chen, Zhihui, 1953– author. | Ko, Joseph H. L., author. |
  Wong, Conrad, author. | Tai, Diamond, author.
Title: Customer needs and strategic management : left-right circles analysis /
  Andrew Chi-fai Chan, The Chinese University of Hong Kong, Hong Kong,
  Joseph H L Ko, Yau Lee Holdings Limited, Hong Kong,
  Conrad Wong, Yau Lee Holdings Limited, Hong Kong,
  Diamond Tai, The Chinese University of Hong Kong, Shenzhen, China.
Description: New Jersey : World Scientific, [2022] | Includes index.
Identifiers: LCCN 2022009702 | ISBN 9789811252884 (hardcover) |
  ISBN 9789811252891 (ebook for institutions) | ISBN 9789811252907 (ebook for individuals)
Subjects: LCSH: Consumer satisfaction. | Customer relations. | Management.
Classification: LCC HF5415.335 .C49 2022 | DDC 658.8/12--dc23/eng/20220405
LC record available at https://lccn.loc.gov/2022009702

British Library Cataloguing-in-Publication Data
A catalogue record for this book is available from the British Library.

For any available supplementary material, please visit
https://www.worldscientific.com/worldscibooks/10.1142/12741#t=suppl

Desk Editors: Aanand Jayaraman/Lixi Dong

Typeset by Stallion Press
Email: enquiries@stallionpress.com

Printed in Singapore

Preface

This is book is titled *Customer Needs and Strategic Management: Left-Right Circles Analysis*. It is a theory that makes use of a simple thinking methodology to delineate the essence of doing business.

This diagrammatic representation of business theory was first conceived almost 30 years ago. It started from this fundamental question: "What does it mean by doing business?"

Using the simplest language, the answer can be: "To use what we are good at to offer something to someone to earn a profit."

Breaking this statement down, it has two components: (i) "To use what we are good at", meaning "using our abilities", or in a more astute manner "deploying our company competences", and (ii) "To offer something to someone to earn a profit", meaning "selling our customers a product or service", or more fundamentally "serving our customer needs".

To place the two elements onto a simple diagram, it displays as two circles: the Left Circle for "Customer Needs" and the Right Circle for "Company Competences". For the customer to buy the company's product or service, it requires the company to pursue the customer needs. That is, the Right Circle pursues the Left Circle for maximum matching.

The perfect scenario is to have the two circles coincide completely, but this does not happen in the real world. The customer has many needs, and not all of them can be satisfied by the company's competences. Hence, only part of the Right Circle can catch up with part of the Left Circle to form an overlapping area called Area C as depicted below.

Chapter 1 of this book gives an overview of the Left-Right Circles structure with its various forms and conditions.

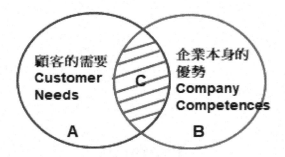

Chapter 2 comes to the most important business concept: Guided by the Left Circle. It is the crucial mindset we need to have in business: Serving the Customer. We have to realize that a company exists only because it has customers. Guided fully by the Left Circle to pursue customer needs, intriguing matching can be made between the Left and Right Circles.

Chapter 3 describes the movements of the two circles: Dynamic Left-Right Circles. Customers are influenced by a lot of factors, including the competitive market, the general environment and its own conditions. The Left Circle will move, and so should the Right Circle in a bid to catch up with the Left Circle. If the Right Circle moves slower than the Left Circle, the company will lose business. If the Right Circle moves at the same pace as the Left Circle, it will maintain its business. If the Right Circle moves faster than the Left Circle in a right way, it will establish a very strong position in the market.

Chapter 4 goes inside the Left Circle and characterizes three levels of existing needs: The old needs of the Old Left Circle, the new needs of the Old Left Circle and the New Left Circle. Understanding these characteristics takes us to higher confidence in satisfying our existing customers, covering other needs of our existing customers, and extending our offerings to new customers.

Chapter 5 indeed takes us back to the Right Circle and instils in us an attitude to treat our own people no less than our customers. Hence, our Internal Left Circle.

Chapter 6 goes to the outer Left Circle and provides a better understanding of how the Left Circle is influenced: Left Circle of Left Circle. The relationship is no longer one-to-one but now one-to-many. It calls for a system approach to understanding the interconnectivity and web of influences and thereby developing initiatives that create impact to the whole system.

Chapter 7 discusses a concept of Turning Left Circle into Right Circle. It goes further in this system approach whereby it makes the customers so satisfied and supportive that they actually become part of the Right Circle that helps enlarge and strengthen the company's ability. This is a very powerful initiative if executed successfully.

Chapter 8 talks about the unrecognized needs of customers. Identifying these unrecognized needs is the key method by which the Right Circle can move faster than the Left Circle to gain a strong market position. Again, it requires a very broad view of the entire system to allow for specific insights to be developed.

Chapter 9 goes even further to the seemingly unrelated Left Circle. While often not a well-designed initiative, capturing this very remote and unapparent Left Circle still counts on using the right perspectives and principles that help yield unexpected results.

Chapter 10 summaries the strategic lesson from this Left-Right Circles theory. It takes four steps in a cycle that is to be repeated:

1. Build upon the past and develop the future — striving to do good work.
2. Take the Left Circle as your guide — with boundless innovation and enhancement.
3. Match the Left and Right Circles — enjoying perfect harmony in what you do.
4. Wallow not in your present success — always looking ahead to the next step.

The 10 chapters complete our Left-Right Circles framework for strategic management. This comes as a result of many years of keen observations and valuable feedback from practical applications. We believe that this is a new and concise angle that deals with business management on a conceptual level. Certainly, like everything else, there can be more to it.

What are the next things we can work on after this framework? There are at least a couple of possibilities.

Firstly, we can gather a lot of practical examples. Over the years, this framework has been taught in our class and discussed in seminars and speeches, with many high-calibre students using it to run their business and conduct other activities. The feedback from the field will be extremely valuable.

Secondly, we believe the Left-Right Circles theory applies not only in business settings but also in personal, family, government, interpersonal and other organizational settings. Particularly in relation to personal aspirations, the different levels of personal needs (reference: Maslow's Hierarchy of Needs) can be matched to this framework, which may help crystalize personal perspectives as far as life planning goes.

These are just a couple of thoughts we have looking ahead to the next step.

About the Authors

Professor Andrew Chi-fai Chan has been invited to be the President of the Greater Bay Area Business School since July 2020. At present, he is also the Emeritus Professor of Department of Marketing in the Chinese University of Hong Kong (CUHK). He was the Director of CUHK EMBA Programme from 2002 to 2020 and Head of Shaw College from 2010 to 2020.

Professor Chan has been active in participating in public services. From 1999 to 2005, he was Chairman of the Hong Kong Consumer Council while from 2004 to 2010, he was Chairman of the Hong Kong Deposit Protection Board; he was also a Member of the Electoral Affairs Commission (2005 to 2012), Chairman of Chinese Medicine Council (2011 to 2017), Council Member of the Hong Kong Institute of Education (2010–2016) and the Hang Seng University of Hong Kong (2007–2019). Currently, he is Chairman of Cantonese Opera Advisory Committee. In addition, he is a Member of Social Enterprise Advisory Committee, Energy Advisory Committee, Cantonese Opera Development Fund Advisory Committee, and Task Force for Review on Enhancement of Lump Sum Grant Subvention System. Besides, he is the Adviser of the Quality Tourism Services Association (QTSA) Governing Council. Professor Chan is also a Member of the College Council of Tung Wah College. In recognition of his distinguished public and community service, he was appointed as a Justice of the Peace in 2005 by the Hong Kong SAR Government and was awarded the Silver Bauhinia Star in 2007.

Joseph H. L. Ko, previously an airline executive in Hong Kong and an independent consultant and entrepreneur in Sydney, Joseph is currently a freelance writer and provides editing and translation services for the Chinese University of Hong Kong from his home in Sydney, Australia.

A graduate from the University of Hong Kong, he obtained an MBA from the University of Michigan, Ann Arbor, USA.

Joseph spent over 17 years at Cathay Pacific in Hong Kong covering various positions in marketing, project management and strategic planning. He also worked 3 years in a travel technology company in Tokyo as Head of Marketing. Arriving in Sydney in 1998, he started his own individual consulting services and received contracts to work for a couple of corporations in Singapore. Influenced by his exposure to entrepreneurship during his MBA studies, he decided in 2004 to turn himself into a small business owner instead. Between 2005 and 2008, he acquired two food service stores in Sydney and managed to achieve significant sales improvements. Being also a part owner of a business brokerage firm, he provides consulting services to help aspiring small business owners with business plans and strategies.

Since 2012, Joseph has been involved in book editing for the EMBA Programme of the Chinese University of Hong Kong. The job keeps him very updated on developments on all fronts around the world. Coupled with his interests in music and football, along with time spent on cultural travels, Joseph has been keeping himself very interested in life.

Ir Dr Conrad Wong is a professional engineer who has over 30 years of building construction experience. He is the Vice-Chairman of Yau Lee Holdings Limited, a listed company in the Hong Kong Stock Exchange (HKEX:0406). A significant building construction group engages in Hong Kong and China markets.

Ir Dr Wong has a passion for green building technologies, Building Information Modeling (BIM), modular and precast construction, and manufacturing automation. Under his leadership, Yau Lee Construction Co. Ltd. has successfully introduced the first concrete Modular Integrated Construction (MiC) in Hong Kong for a government quarter project. Since 2017, Ir Dr Wong has put a great deal of effort into developing various robotic and Artificial Intelligence (A.I.) applications for the construction industry.

Currently, Ir Dr Wong is the Deputy Chairman of the Council of the Hong Kong Metropolitan University, the Member of the Energy Advisory

Committee and the Member of the Town Planning Board. In the past, Ir Dr Wong served as the Deputy Chairman of Vocational Training Council, the Chairman of the Occupational Safety and Health Council, the Chairman of the Hong Kong Green Building Council, the President of the Hong Kong Construction Association and the Director of the World Green Building Council.

Ir Dr Wong was awarded the "2001 Hong Kong Outstanding Young Digi Persons Award" and the "Bauhinia Cup Outstanding Entrepreneur Award 2002" presented by the Hong Kong Polytechnic University. In 2009, he was conferred the Honorary Fellow by the Vocational Training Council and the Honorary Fellow by the University of Central Lancashire to recognise his contributions.

Ir Dr Wong was a member of the 10th and 11th Guizhou Province Committee of the Chinese People's Political Consultative Conference. He was appointed Justice of the Peace (J.P.) in 2008 and awarded the Bronze Bauhinia Star (B.B.S.) by the Government of the HKSAR in the year 2013 for recognition of his outstanding contributions made to the Construction Industry.

Dr. Diamond Tai, currently Adjunct Associate Professor at the Chinese University of Hong Kong (Shenzhen), is experienced in teaching Marketing and Advertising courses, and focusing on the development of marketing strategies in the Greater Bay Area. Dr. Tai has been serving the advertising industry in China and Hong Kong for more than 30 years. When he started his career in advertising, he was the first batch of practitioner in China advertising. He is a seasoned strategic and practical advertising practitioner. He has supported many international 4A advertising companies to land in China and introduced newcomers into the industry.

Now Dr. Tai is operating his independent advertising company, serving customer brands at home and abroad. In addition to analyzing and discussing contemporary marketing theories and practices, he and his mentor, Professor Andrew CF Chan, co-authored "Left and Right Circles — Holistic Strategy Analysis", which can also be applied to individuals, family, workplace, interpersonal relationships and other fields, and serves as a reference for different readers.

Contents

Introduction

Often, "Customer First", or even "Customer as the Sole Purpose", has been touted as the golden principle to conduct business in our commercial world. But to a lot of people, practising it is not as simple as it sounds. People go their own ways to interpret the principle and take on different approaches in practice.

In this book, we develop a "Left-Right Circles" theory where we put customer needs as the "Left Circle". We analyze the various levels of customer needs and the key approaches to satisfying those needs. Further, a company has to develop its own strengths as competencies, represented by the "Right Circle" in this theory. We describe how the Left and Right Circles interact, moving in sync in a perfectly harmonious manner, offering products and services that customers will repeatedly purchase, thereby building a strong base of loyal supporters for the company.

To let readers grasp the significance of the whole "Left-Right Circles" theory, we have included the various levels of needs in the 10 chapters of this book. A full detailed discussion with practical examples of each level is given in each chapter to allow readers to take in what they believe is useful for their practice.

The Left Circle-driven approaches are equally applicable to serving customers and serving stakeholders. The approaches apply effectively to non-profit organizations as well as to companies. The theory is also applicable to dealing with interpersonal situations, enabling relationships to grow closer and stronger. These approaches help us bring harmony and joy to all aspects of our lives.

Chapter 1

What is "Left-Right Circles"?: Overview of Left-Right Circles with Areas A To E

The "Left-Right Circles" theory is composed of two parts. Put simply, the Left Circle denotes "Customer Needs" while the Right Circle represents "Company Competences". The company must utilize its capabilities to the utmost to satisfy these customer needs.

Figure 1 shows the simplest form of Left-Right Circles. In the diagram, Area C is where a company has to pursue continuously. It is where the customer needs and company competences intersect, essentially being where business success lies. Area A denotes where customers have other needs, but these needs are not met by the existing company competences. Yet, this is also where the company can seek further development. Conversely, Area B denotes where the company has certain other capabilities, but these characteristics are not required by the customers. Investing time and other resources in this area is deemed a waste of the company's scarce resources, bringing no benefits at all to the business.

Left Circle Needs

Let us first discuss the Left Circle. People doing business need to consider the Left Circle first and foremost. At this point, we take the Left Circle as to represent needs of the target customers (but it also includes the needs of other groups which we will discuss later). Human beings have different

1

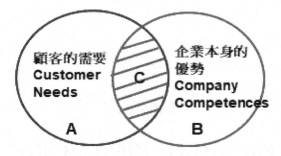

Figure 1:   Left-Right Circles — basic diagram.

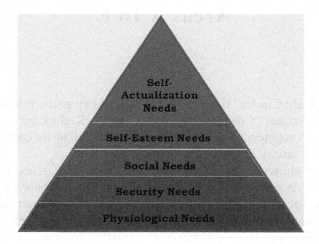

Figure 2:   Maslow's hierarchy of needs.

needs. As illustrated in Figure 2 (Maslow's hierarchy of needs), Abraham Maslow, the American psychologist, classifies human needs as to have five different levels: physiological needs (such as food, water and air), security needs (such as a stable life), social needs (such as friendships), esteem needs (such as genuine respect from others) and self-actualization needs (such as realizing potentials beyond one's own expectation).

Clothing, food, housing and transportation are basic life essentials. However, even within these basic physiological needs, there contain higher-level needs. Let us look at clothing. Tracing back to the original intent, we ask what needs the sellers are trying to satisfy when they sell clothes. As a basic function, clothes provide shelter for the body, keep us warm and give us protection. Above this, clothing is indeed a part of how we look. Why do we put ourselves in formal suits when we go to important meetings? We have to observe social norms.

This means that "clothing" has gone above the basic function of protection and evolved into a signal of respect, a way of self-expression and a part of the social norm. For when you wish to appease someone you fancy, you would certainly choose your outfit very carefully. How you dress is indeed a good reflection of your personality. For clothing alone, there are myriad needs to satisfy. Successful sellers would thoroughly understand all motives in buying and choose where they set their targets to satisfy the inherent needs.

Next, we look at food. Apart from filling up, a basic need for food is a balanced nutrition. In addition, food consumers are concerned about food safety. They want to know if the food is fully cooked, if it has been contaminated, and even where the food is consumed, such as if the food is exposed to dirt and dust, or disease-carrying insects. Not only need the stomach be filled but the food has to be hygienic as well.

To go a step further, why do you favour a certain eatery above the others which are equally capable of filling you up and are also safe? You may simply favour a certain restaurant for its quiet ambience while dining. Apart from food, the environment can be a need to be satisfied. If you are dining out with your friend, his preference is also in your consideration. If your friend is a vegan, taking him to have meat or seafood is a violation of the very basic social etiquette and respect.

Related to that is another need: what you eat and how you eat can also be a symbol of your status or a sign of how you respect the others. Take the example of Monkey King in the old Chinese novel *Journey to the West*. He storms into heaven wanting to savour the "Queen Mother Peach". Is the peach particularly tasty? Perhaps it is, but he has no idea about it beforehand. What is the most valuable to Monkey King is probably the fact that the peach is difficult to get. The drive behind his action probably comes from the sense of achievement that he will get, which is where the real need is. The peach to Monkey King is a 5-caret diamond to an ordinary person. The value of the diamond comes from its rarity. Not everyone can afford to buy it, so it offers a sense of superiority to the customer who can afford it.

For "a roof above our heads", what needs are to be satisfied in housing? We of course do not want a noisy environment which will disturb our sleep and peaceful living. Our health will be adversely affected if we live amidst polluted air. These are a couple of basic needs. The issue of where to live also has a social dimension. All of us are social animals. We may choose a certain place because it is close to our friends. Others may take priority in whether the place is within the catchment area of a certain school they desire for their children, over and above other considerations such as the quality of the building and ease of transportation. Property developers are certainly conscious of those needs when they bid for a certain piece of land.

As regards transportation, different people choose different means to travel over a route. Some go after speed, while others take ticket prices very seriously. Some older people seek nostalgic moments to travel on the tram, taking opportunities to reminisce the old faces of Sheung Wan, Central, Wanchai and the like. To ensure arriving on time, some people travelling for a meeting would rather take the train than risk being stuck in traffic jams with taxi, even though they have no affordability issue.

The Left Circle is not all that straightforward. We also see people prefer using the bicycle, for the cause of preserving the environment and keeping the air clean. This is the mode of transportation that also offers the benefit of physical exercise along with environmental protection, thereby becoming a way to demonstrate one's own temperament and atti-tude. Over time, it can develop into a social norm or culture, just as people in Europe increasingly adopt it as their preferred way of getting around. This being the case, still there are people who simply go cycling for the sake of reminiscing their childhood days with parents.

Noting that all different behaviours exist, we should never approach transportation as a single need. Left Circle considerations are not as sim-ple as we may think. Should we take people's need as "getting there" only, then blocking all train windows with advertisements will be a serious mistake as we will find people not happy with their sight being obscured even when they can get to their destination easily. We need to take a com-plete view in assessing the Left Circle needs.

If we conduct our business activities based only on the Right Circle (the company's competences and qualities) without assessing the Left Circle, what results can we expect? We have a counterexample. A mobile phone manufacturer had rolled out a super-small phone set, a palm-sized device that includes a keyboard. Technically, it was superb craftsmanship. But apart from those with super small hands, no one else was able to use it. Not surprisingly, the product has become a flop.

Another example is related to the Hong Kong HOS flats where the government first made sinks and toilets as standard installations when they sold the flats. Yet it was found that many buyers did not like those products, so they replaced them later with the ones of their liking. It started as a good intention from the government but ultimately resulted in a lot of wastes. On the other hand, builders in Taiwan would give buyers a choice upfront as to whether to install these facilities, and the cost would be reimbursed back to the buyers should they opt for their own installations. In this way, different needs in the Left Circle are looked after.

Right Circle Competences

On the Left Circle needs, we need to properly sense them, respect them and respond to them. If not, results would not come. Then, what makes the Right Circle crucial? As we come to realize the Left Circle needs, we will need corresponding Right Circle capabilities to meet and satisfy them. What is your company capable of doing? What your company can do is indeed your Right Circle, which determines if you company is able to meet the Left Circle needs.

In fact, when assessing the Left Circle needs, you need to take into account your Right Circle capabilities. I will go into the clothing, food, housing and transportation examples again for illustration.

Firstly, clothing. These days people expect a jacket capable of shielding rain as well as dispersing heat. Do you have such techniques? If you do not, then those Left Circle needs are not your targets. When the Left Circle and the Right Circle are too far apart, whatever effort you put in will be to no avail. If you already know how to make the jacket water-resistant, then you may just delve into studying how to make it breathable as well. This will make your Right Circle much stronger, enabling you to roll out a suitable product that satisfies the Left Circle needs.

To get to a new level of competence, companies need to invest into building new skills and capabilities through research and development, thereby bringing positive effects to the world of innovation. The most direct benefit is that customers in the Left Circle get what they want, and the transactions make positive contributions to society. Different styles of outfit have different admirers of their own, and your customers favour your products because you are capable of meeting their needs.

Next, food. How do we see the Right Circle working in terms of food? Food safety is certainly the very basic Right Circle standard for a restaurant. Beyond safety, some restaurants lure customers by appealing to their taste buds, often offering intense flavours in the form of rich and oily foods. But this approach addresses the taste category only, overlooking the demand for healthy food. In the Left Circle, the demand for healthy food is increasing by the day. If you ignore this demand altogether, not offering any healthy alternatives, you are simply rejecting those kinds of customers.

What you can do is to strengthen your Right Circle by adding several healthy choices, such as a vegetarian menu, so customers can enjoy a wider selection. Your coverage of the Left Circle becomes more comprehensive, with expected benefits to your business along with more satisfied customers. Apart from food itself, location, ambience and service levels are also part of the Right Circle offerings. Should the owner have very good connections with celebrities, the reputation of his restaurant can be quite lifted by such links. In that sense, his social network constitutes a very strong Right Circle element.

After clothing and food, what should we know about the Right Circle as related to a place to live? Housing suppliers today are not limited to commercial firms, with the government and NGOs also providing for housing needs. Even some social enterprises are playing their roles as housing providers for the underprivileged. Given this, applications of Left-Right Circles are certainly not confined to the commercial world. While all are housing suppliers one way or another, they do have different ways to respond to housing needs in the Left Circle.

Some commercial developers concentrate on supplying for high-end buyers. Their products usually feature magnificent views and use of top-class materials, and not surprisingly, carry high price tags too. In contrast, to the ordinary people living in government housing estates, the relevant housing designs need to be practical yet easy to maintain. To cater for different Left Circle needs, different professional teams are deployed by different suppliers to exercise their relevant Right Circle competences.

The Right Circle in the transportation sector contains an even wider array of business focuses. Many different companies offer travel services. Take the example of airlines. One airline portrays itself as delivering good service, and it needs to build a whole service culture throughout the company to back it up. Another airline sets its selling point in safety, and it needs to make excellent choices in aircraft types and maintenance works. All these are their respective Right Circle competences.

Quite a few low-cost airlines entered the market recently, and their Left Circle customers are mainly those travelling on a low budget. Executives travelling on company business are apparently not their targets, and as such, these low-cost airlines are less inclined to make on-time performance their Right Circle advantage compared with the full-service airlines.

Generally speaking, companies can use three methods to strengthen their Right Circle advantages. The first is operation efficiency, which means relying on fast and economical ways to deliver reliable services and products. The second is customer intimacy, which is to use brand and customer relationship as the business main thrust. This includes a lot of companies now utilizing the ever more popular big data analytics to develop strong knowledge about customers. The last is product leadership, which is to offer innovative and market leading products. Apple is a classic example of this as a leading technology company.[1]

For the business to prosper, companies need to understand the Left Circle and the Right Circle thoroughly. Your business not doing well has undesirable consequences: your customers do not get their desired products and services, your employees' livelihood is hard-hit, your investors have their money down the drain, and your suppliers are unable to recover their debts. In the treatment of Left-Right Circles, not only the customers, but the employees, investors and business partners are also part of the Left Circle. Companies need to look after all stakeholders' interests. We will discuss this in more detail in later chapters.

But overall, we cannot take Left-Right Circles management lightly, as your mistakes jeopardize not only yourself but also others. The rippling effect can be serious.

Meeting Point of Left and Right Circles

Let us define Left-Right Circles in greater depth. The Left Circle represents the customers you choose to serve. They have different needs. Those needs include some they know they have and others they do not even recognize they have. What you need to do is to identify and understand

---

[1] Michael Treacy and Fred Wiersma, 1997, *The Discipline of Market Leaders.*

these needs, and choose which ones you want to satisfy. You do not have to cover all the needs, because in the world of diverse needs, we can count on a model of "division of labour". You look at where your skills and expertise lie, and choose from the Left Circle the categories of needs that you believe your strengths and advantages are best suited for delivering a solution. If you do not see a meeting point between the Left and Right Circles, there will be no business to talk of. You have to have a very clear view in this judgement, or else there will be very little that you can achieve.

There are formidable competitors in the market. Why do you think you are still the one that can deliver a solution for the needs you have chosen to satisfy? That is because of the superior way your Left and Right Circles meet. This can be down to the fact that you have better experience in the subject matter. Or, the services you design fit the bill better. Or, your ideas are more innovative, so your image stands out. Or, you have a service package complementing the product, and the customers like it better. These are all your Right Circle specialities, and they overlap nicely with the Left Circle needs.

From this, we can see that the Right Circle is not about products only, and the Left Circle does not merely include customers. You need to satisfy other people too such as your staff. This is the concept of "Internal Left Circle", which we will explain in Chapter 5. If you cannot grasp all the intricacies in Left-Right Circles, you will not be able to execute to the best result. Your whole endeavour will be far from perfect.

The Left-Right Circles concept comes directly as your *raison d'être*. What is your *raison d'être*? It is your ability to deliver a solution to solve problems for other people in the context of satisfying their needs. You have your own unique ability in this world. While others are doing their utmost to find the best overlap spots in their Left and Right Circles, yours can be the most precise and intricate. If there is no in-depth analysis from Left-Right Circles, it would be difficult to craft out a clear vision and effective strategies for the next 3, 5 or 10 years. Analysis from Left-Right Circles does not only concern the Left Circle needs today but also the changes that we expect in, say, the next 3 years and beyond.

At the same time, competition is also changing. You may choose to strengthen your Right Circle abilities so that you can compete head-on with your rivals. Should your competitors show they have abilities in certain thing, you can differentiate yourself by doing it faster. Should they be fast enough, you can improve your quality. You can also choose to target another group in the Left Circle, just as when somebody goes for fine dining, you go for fast food. Yet another choice is to do different things in the same category, choosing to go upstream when others are doing midstream or downstream, or *vice versa*. Taking the example of fast food, if somebody is already doing a great job in service, you can engage yourself in back-end food processing. If somebody is already doing food processing, then you can well be a supplier of fresh produce.

While people may compete with one another, they can work on their respective areas of excellence and excel where they work best. In this way, they can even be mutually supportive of one another. When someone has worked out the applicable software for emergency alarm, you can set yourself to provide the supporting call-centre service. When both hardware and software have been sufficiently provided, you can offer training services for staff. Or, if you believe your capability is up for it, then you can do research for the next-generation product.

Competition need not be a life and death matter, and competitors can indeed give each other due respect for co-existence. After all, the world is constantly changing, and there is always a new way that you can look up to. As new technologies are emerging at a very fast pace these days, needs are changing equally fast. The Left Circle you have been serving well will surely require something new.

Many people are unclear about their *raison d'être* as a business. Some declare that they have a very big and strong company. But for what reasons do they want their company to be big and strong? If huge financial backing and an immense structure are what they consider as making their company strong, the question is whether these are the elements that meet the Left Circle needs. Let us say, yours is a company that sells high-tech products, and your Left Circle customers expect you to roll out products with delightful new features. Your company size is not what they see as important. If your large size would instead slow you down on product introduction, then size ironically becomes a weakness. So, when some think they possess strengths that only benefit very few people on the Left Circle, they may be well short of an ability to satisfy all crucial needs there.

Your *raison d'être* will change with time. While it may be that your company used to build its strength on a comprehensive database, you may suddenly find this redundant as powerful search engines exist now to provide instant accessibility via online search. Your Right Circle strengths that served you well may apply no longer. Your expertise may have been in accounting. But these days your job can be totally replaced by automated accounting applications. Not too long ago, there were text copyists. They took pride in precise transcription and elegant calligraphy. Yet, the copy machine had taken all these advantages away.

Perhaps you were good in teaching with great knowledge in certain subjects. But these days about 60–70% of the relevant knowledge is available on the internet, and the value of coming to your class has diminished significantly. The same Right Circle does not draw the same admiration anymore. As a teacher, you cannot just focus on passing on general knowledge alone. Rather, you need to add insights to the subjects, or come into cross-disciplinary and cross-cultural areas in your studies, adapting your teaching to a Chinese environment, for example. The key is to seek uniqueness in what you do, keeping an edge that makes you competitive.

Thinking that your Right Circle strengths can serve you forever without responding to the changing Left Circle needs can be the biggest mistake of all. As Lao Tzu said, "Disaster lurks within good fortune." Your strength today can be your weakness tomorrow. Small-sized companies can count on good flexibility, high commitment and strong sense of crisis as their strengths. Large-sized companies often fall into the trap of getting further and further away from the Left Circle. Their complex structure and fine division of responsibilities are weakening their sensitivity to market changes. This could well be the biggest threat to their future. In recent years, the rise of Tesla has been deemed the biggest threat to the traditional carmakers. It is amazing to see a new market entrant like Tesla leading the way to an electric car future.

Left-Right Circles Basic Diagram

We have captured the entire Left-Right Circles theory in Figure 3.

The Left Circle contains various needs; the Right Circle contains various competences. When certain competences are able to satisfy certain needs, the Left and Right Circles overlap. The Left Circle has two areas: Area A and Area C. The Right Circle also has two areas: Area B and Area C. Area A is where those Left Circle needs are not satisfied by the Right Circle competences. Area B is where those Right Circle competences are not needed by the Left Circle. Area C is the overlapping area. This is where the Left Circle needs and the Right Circle competences coincide.

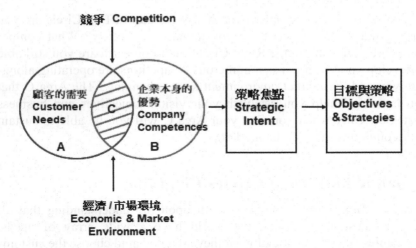

Figure 3:   Complete Left-Right Circles diagram.

It is where the Left Circle needs are satisfied by what the Right Circle offers in terms of products and personnel.

Area C is the most important part. The area represents the value of the business and why the business exists. Commercially, this overlapping area is where the all-important business transactions take place. Understanding the reasons of the overlap (i.e. why our competences can meet the needs), we can conceive our development plans for the next 5–10 years. We can adjust our products and personnel to better target the Left Circle. With such a vision, we can move forward confidently to realize our objectives, short- and medium-term. This is the epitome of the whole Left-Right Circles theory.

The overlapping of the Left and Right Circles is also affected by competition and the general business environment. When the market environment changes and new competitors emerge, needs also change in the Left Circle. It will become necessary that you adjust your objectives and strategies accordingly. Just as in the 1980s when the Chinese mainland adopted an opening policy, it caused an immense change to the Hong Kong market environment. Numerous factories in Hong Kong had moved north to achieve a lower-cost position. It would almost be a requirement to follow this direction, or else one would find it difficult to maintain a foothold in the market. But for those who took up the trend earlier, they might see their business volume increase manifold.

Now, you need to ponder over this: What sort of Left Circle are you serving today? What needs are you targeting to satisfy? What competences are you using in the Right Circle? Why on earth are you still able to develop your Area C when numerous competitors are operating alongside you and the market environment keeps changing? The Area C that you have will help you establish your vision, objectives and business strategies. Only when you find your Area C will you be able to sustain your competitiveness in the market.

Dynamic Left-Right Circles Diagram

The Left-Right Circles theory is built upon the understanding that all kinds of customers around the world have a wide array of needs. Companies take advantage of what they are good at to choose the customers and the needs they want to satisfy. While doing this, they need to understand the general business climate reflecting the economic, social, environmental, technological and political environments. Certainly, they need to understand their competitors too. If your competitors can do much better than you, perhaps you should not select this particular Left Circle to compete.

That does not mean that you have to do a complete change. What you probably have to do is to make a certain adjustment. Even for certain Left Circle groups that have very close needs, their needs are still different.

Consider this example. You are a tailor making suits amidst a whole host of famous brands also making suits. The competition is intense. But you can focus on making suits for graduates who need suitable outfits for job interviews. What kind of suits do they need? Which grade of suits is needed for the purpose? The suits definitely need to look decent even though we can expect the graduates to be very price sensitive. Targeting this group, your price level has to be reasonable and affordable. But the important point is that the style of your suits needs to be of good taste not looking "cheap". While people may recognize that it is not the top brands, they still see it as befitting the status of a graduate.

This can avoid more luxurious brands from trading down to compete with you. It is not that no one will ever want to compete, but when you have taken up a leading position in the market, they will think twice before deciding to go head-on with you. It is likely that they would rather do customized suits for customers with higher spending power. In fact, many customers require special customization to fit their non-standard body shapes and sizes, and this can be yet another avenue by which to establish a market niche.

Area C

After you have found your target market, Area C emerges. Using Left-Right Circles to analyze your business prospect, you first identify some needs in the Left Circle which you wish to serve. After reviewing your competitors and the general environment, you move your Right Circle towards the needs you have identified. The area where the Left and Right Circles meet is Area C — those Left Circle needs that can be satisfied.

However, the area where the Left Circle does not overlap with the Right Circle (Area A) is also very important. It indicates there are still a lot of needs that have yet to coincide with your Right Circle advantages. On the other hand, the part in your Right Circle that does not coincide with the Left Circle (Area B) represents your other advantages that have yet found a suitable market for applications. These advantages may be superb in your own eyes, but they are not the ones favoured by your Left Circle customers.

As such, Area C is still the most important to you. The market has needs, and you can satisfy them. This is the reason why you are in the market. You ought to do your best to maintain your Area C. If you have not yet landed an Area C, you have to conceive one and develop it. But once you have landed one, you still have to monitor if there are any changes. You have to adjust your strategies and build your corresponding Right Circle strengths to cater for the changes as you find them. This is the essence of Dynamic Left-Right Circles, which we will explain below in more detail using a few diagrams.

I have shown the Left-Right Circles theory in a diagram in Figure 3. But that is only a static view. Figure 4 starts showing movements of Left-Right Circles. Compared with Figure 3, Area C in Figure 4 has shrunk following movement of the Left Circle to the left. What has happened is that needs in the Left Circle change all the time and are moving away from your competences in the Right Circle. It may be because your customers have used your services and are expecting even better ones, such as higher quality, lower price or more functions.

It is natural that people have an insatiable desire for something better. If you simply stay where you are, you will be unable to satisfy these ever-changing needs, thereby putting yourself on a path to redundancy

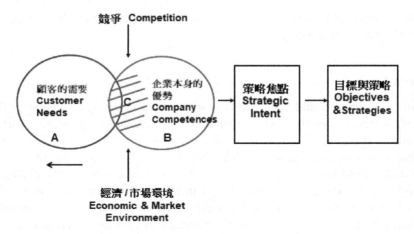

Figure 4:   Area C has shrunk because the Left Circle has moved left.

eventually. That is when the Left Circle will move further and further away from you. While you may be doing very well in your existing Area C, your competitors will certainly do their utmost in a bid to take a share from you. This sort of intense competition may get your Left Circle to move away. As a result, your Area C will shrink, and you will find it increasingly difficult to maintain your business. As your Left Circle tends also to expand, there should be more needs for you to target. However, it is just that you will find yourself having very limited capabilities to go after these needs.

A company often has no awareness of its Left Circle moving away, and thus the business declines. In his book *How the Mighty Fall*, author Jim Collins said, "Every institution is vulnerable, no matter how great. No matter how much you've achieved, no matter how far you've gone, no matter how much power you've garnered, you're vulnerable to decline." Every so often, it is just because their Left Circle has left, but companies still retain a deep love of their own Right Circle, self-pityingly complaining about everything else including their disloyal customers, price-cutting competitors, the changed environment or even bad luck. But the world does not operate as they wish. The Left Circle will definitely leave you behind — it is just a matter of time. What you need to do is to make the right changes to your Right Circle to catch up with the Left Circle.

Nokia is a classic example. They have been the leader of the mobile phone market but have ignored the emerging trend of smartphones without developing any products in that regard. As a result, they have just

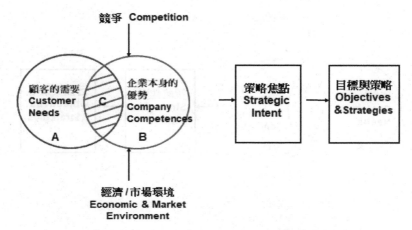

Figure 5: Area C of the same size but with different contents.

surrendered the whole market to Apple and Samsung within a few short years.

Figure 5 appears to be the same as Figure 3, but it has indeed undergone changes. The Left Circle has moved more to the left, and the Right Circle has followed it and caught up with the new needs. The Area C in Figure 5 is new and is different from that in Figure 3 because it has embraced the new needs.

We go back to the earlier example of carmakers. Now that consumers have a higher level of awareness in environmental issues, there are increasing demands for electric cars in the market. Almost all traditional carmakers have now invested substantial resources in developing new battery technologies, with a view to rolling out their own electric cars as early as possible. This is how the world moves on. You are constantly being influenced by the competition and by other factors such as the economy, the market, technology advances and environmental concerns. If you can follow the changes and get yourself up with the new needs in the Left Circle, you should at least be able to maintain your position in the market.

Area D

Can you go faster than the Left Circle? Take a look at Figure 6. In Area A, there are needs that you are unable to fulfil at the moment. This is not your territory as yet. Still, you should contemplate building your Area D.

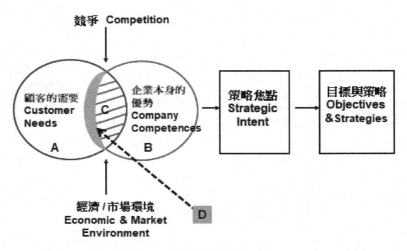

Figure 6:   Birth of Area D.

It is where those customers are not yet yours because you are not fulfilling their needs, but they are very close to your Right Circle. What you can do is to try to build a new territory there. This is how strategies come about. Strategies are to consider what to do and what not to do. What not to do is Area B. What to do is going towards Area A. Of course, Area A is a wide area, and you cannot do everything that Area A demands. But there are things that are close enough to your capabilities. This indeed is Area D.

Will it be a sure win to build an Area D? All strategic moves carry risks. But when Area D is close to your capabilities in the Right Circle, it indicates that you are more able, and thus have a higher chance of success, than your competitors in satisfying those needs. While you are adjusting yourself to cater for those external changes, the Right Circle that you move to develop further capabilities involves something you should already have some good understanding of. The way you move for the new needs should be well within your grasp.

If your strengths have been in computer technology, you would be the first to notice the change in the market and the trends towards Big Data, CRM and network technology. You would be the first to acquire the relevant knowledge and skills for the new Area D. Your speed of development and your chance of success should be higher than your competitors'. You would have better capabilities to establish a firm foothold in this territory. The biggest risk, however, is that you are unable or reluctant to identify Area D, allowing yourself to wallow in the comforting thoughts of your good old days and constantly reminiscing how good your business has been. Unfortunately, this kind of standing-still complacency will see the Left Circle leaving you behind and your business dwindling.

Area E

Lastly, we also have an Area E. What is it? When the Left Circle moves away from you, a part of Area C will become Area B. This area used to be the area of your advantage, but times have changed. What used to be your advantage has now been replaced by new products and customers have left you for those products. The glory that you attained from this category has been consigned to history.

Management guru Peter Drucker has put forward a concept of "planned abandonment", advocating a purposeful and orderly abandonment of outdated activities in a business. If you are not eliminating these low-value activities, your valuable resources will continue to be taken up by them with your rescue effort yielding no result. The focus of your effort, which should instead be on what the market needs, will be weakened by these unproductive activities.

Consultant firm Boston Consulting Group (BCG) classifies business brands into four categories: Question Marks, Stars, Cash Cows and Dogs. If your certain brand has reached the level of "Dogs", it tells you that it is no longer favoured by the market and has no future. Continuing it means a waste of time and effort by management and staff. Those past glories of yours belong to Area E. You have to constantly review if Area E exists in your company so you can take action to discard it accordingly. An example is this divestment of business is the production halt of typewriters and copying machines at IBM.

You have to eliminate Area E and expand Area D as shown in Figure 7. That is, you have to discard what is not needed any more and capture the new needs of the market. Even wiser is to foresee the market trends and identify what will become your Area E. You will start early to reduce activities in this area. If you remain stubbornly stuck to the activities, you will be powerless to save the situation when your entire Area C has turned into Area E. We should always get ourselves prepared for changes when our Area C is still strong. What we need to do is to expand Area D and eliminate Area E when identified.

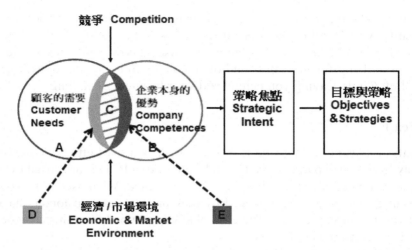

Figure 7:   Companies need to expand Area D but eliminate Area E.

Looking back at the blossoming wig industry in Hong Kong in the 1960s and 1970s, we saw forward-looking industrialists quickly moving over to real estate as they started to realize the changing habits of the US consumers. Many people saw their actions as crazy at the time, but ultimately they were proven to be visionary.

When you have successfully captured an Area D, it will become your new core business in Area C. This is the time when you have to conceive new D2 plans, your new wave of Area D. This is what a company should do consistently, as demonstrated in the dynamic Left-Right Circles diagram. In Mr. Li Ka-shing's group of businesses, real estate has always been the mainstay. But there have been consistent efforts to expand into new lines of business in port management, telecommunications, energy and infrastructure. Every now and then, there is a new Area D emerging, effectively building it up to an empire of diverse businesses that he currently owns.

Left-Right Circles in Various Sectors

Some people would ask, "We are not running a business. Does the Left-Right Circles concept apply to us?" Let us examine it through four professions: administrators, farmers, workers and business owners/managers.

For "administrators", we are referring to the government officials or civil servants. How do they see their *raison d'être*? Do they have a Left

Circle? They do, of course. All citizens, along with the next generation including babies not yet born, are their Left Circle. They have to consider whether their policies will have an undesirable effect in exhausting public resources or polluting the environment. They need to be mindful of what kind of society their policies will leave — the culture and the value system. Will it turn the society into one that is dominated by money with people chasing wealth by whatever means? Or will there be a strong sense of civic responsibility and mutual respect within the community bringing about balance and harmony? All these are mandates for policymakers and government officials.

The administrators' Left Circle is not confined to their superiors. If they only work for getting approvals from the higher-ups, they would be locked in a very shallow way of thinking, unable to fulfil the significance of Left-Right Circles. As ones who work for the interests of the public, they should put themselves in the shoes of the people and realize any potential issues and concerns before the people are aware of them. This gives them the opportunity to work on the solutions early. They will be happy when the people are happy. This is much like Sir Winston Churchill who first saw the ambitions of Hitler before the Second World War and made full preparations for war against the Nazis. His early detection of the danger led the UK to final victory.

So much so about the Left Circle for administrators, then what is their Right Circle? Government officials need to be very much "down-to-earth". They need to be well-informed and have empathy for the people. They need to be well-conversant with how different issues are handled by countries around the world, which they take as references. They need to have a perspective of what the needs are for the next generation — the future Left Circle, so-to-speak. More closely, they need to keep abreast of all social trends and developments, a full picture of the entire social fabric.

On the subject of waste management, officials need to have a vision of the situation for 5–10 years later. If they have no idea about methods such as reduction at source and upcycling, then they have a very questionable Right Circle. Perhaps 20 years ago, they were recruited on the basis of their excellent academic qualifications, good command of English and logical thinking capabilities. But if their Right Circle has shown no improvements since, detached from what is actually happening, not only are they unqualified to serve but they are holding back the entire population — their Left Circle.

For example, some countries are stuck in their old rail facilities, unable to catch up with those that have switched to the latest systems. They lag behind so much that they even have difficulties meeting basic safety standards. Their Right Circle has remained stationary for so long, while the Left Circle has moved further and further away from them.

After the officials and administrators, we will talk about the "farmers". Agriculture is important, but there are places where farming for some crops is difficult, such as for corns. But why are corns a requirement of the Left Circle? Is it because of the nutrition value or just taste and texture? Are there any alternatives? If you are able to open your mind up and get deep into this sort of thinking process, then you are not a farmer like any other and can do a lot more than the rest.

The farming sector has competition too. So, how do you make yourself stand out in this competition? You will have to have a clear mind about which processes to revolutionize and which traditions to keep. In more advanced countries, agriculture has embraced the use of data to analyze farming methods, so as to introduce high-precision seeding and irrigation processes thereby getting more abundant harvests.

Next, we discuss the "workers". What products should the workers make? What are their quality standards? Say, a customer asks for 20,000 nails to be shipped to him. The factory manufactures the nails using its usual "minimum cost" principle, but the products may not meet what the customer in the Left Circle wants. If the customer wants these nails for some special purposes, then the nails delivered are simply rendered useless. The factory has to be very clear about these: Which Left Circle customers are they serving? What purposes are these nails planned to be used for?

Many factories are just a small part of the whole production value chain. Normally, they cannot see the forest for the trees, and thus are a distance away from the requirement of the Left Circle. That is why Dr. W. Edwards Deming, the quality management guru, made a point about "breaking down barriers" so as to allow information to flow through both upper and lower streams of the value chain, or between departments of the same company, so that all parts can act as one and be close to the Left Circle.

You have to put yourself in the positions of the Left Circle and realize what needs all your "customers" have. To be responsible for packaging, you have to consider a lot of factors: Apart from making it attractive, does it offer good protection to the product? Would it cause difficulties to distribution and delivery? This is related to your business partners in transportation and is a part of the factory's Left Circle — your "customers". If you fail to take everything into consideration, you will regret for all the slip-ups that you may have to front up with in the market. What is important is that you think seriously beforehand about all the requirements of your Left Circle.

This thorough consideration may take you to a different insight so that you might decide that you would rather produce another product. A Japanese company producing CD-ROMs has faced the issue of the Left Circle moving away. The market was gradually moving away from CD-ROMs, but they realized that the core technology in the product was the laser transmitter. So, they transferred this technology to the production of fingerprint readers, opening up a new line of business at the end.

Finally, it is back to business. From the very beginning of this book, we have been discussing many Left-Right Circles cases. But here we talk about not only the transactions but the social missions behind these commercial transactions. The fact that you have provided your Left Circle with what they want to buy with the quality they want has given them a certain level of satisfaction. This has led to you earning your money due and your customers enjoying some form of satisfaction with the products that they have purchased.

In addition, having a well-run company means you are looking after your employees, as well as your upstream suppliers. When your business is doing really well, you will give your good employees bonuses, thereby improving their livelihood. As you may also expand your business and put in additional investments, you are contributing to the entire economy. Your business may only be a small part of the economy, but as every business is doing its own part in line with the Left-Right Circles principles, the entire community will benefit from these thriving businesses. Business is therefore not only about making money but should encompass a cause towards social well-being to individuals and the community as a whole.

The business world is a complicated one. As in the Left-Right Circles theory, your business focus is in Area C where your strengths and abilities can be used to satisfy needs of your target Left Circle customers. You will have some other abilities too (Area B), but you should guard against expending too much time and energy on this area, as those abilities do not point to what the Left Circle needs. Area A is the portion of the Left Circle you are unable to satisfy now, but if you see an opportunity of extending your abilities to cover some part of this, it is certainly worth your effort trying.

You need to also watch the competition and monitor if someone else is doing better and cheaper than you. If so, the question for you is: are your resources better deployed elsewhere than being used to fight this battle? While having developed a Left-Right Circles blueprint to guide your whole company, including the departments, and even your industry, to success, you still need to keep up with the global trends for change and constantly push yourself towards higher levels.

In the education sector, for example, students today are not in the classroom to take up knowledge only, but their learning and development can also be through a network of peers interacting with each other. The alumni group that they will be a part of come graduation may turn out to be a great asset in their future career.

If a school "sells" only a certificate, then its curriculum can hardly be considered as great. A few teachers want always to teach their favourite subjects only, caring little about the students' ability to grasp the ideas, a typical attitude that has a focus on Area B only. At the same time, Area A is often ignored. Students may find no help available as they seek assistance after class. These needs, while important, are ignored. It is not to say that teachers do not have the liberty to dedicate their time to upgrading their knowledge, but delivering the needed services has to be their first priority.

To sum up the whole chapter, we can see a very wide application of the Left-Right Circles theory across all industries and professions, and certainly it is not confined to the business sector.

The Origin of Left-Right Circles

How was the theory of Left-Right Circles first conceived? An organization invited a professor to give a lecture in 1992. But the organization had a request. The head of personnel asked, "Professor, can you tone down the theoretical side of your lecture so that it can relate better to the real business world?" The professor asked himself, "Would it be possible to consolidate all the business wisdom that I want to pass on into one simple diagram for easy understanding?" This is the origin of Left-Right Circles.

Almost 30 years since the lecture, this Left-Right Circles theory has been helping us to explain this complex world of business transactions, in terms of the strategies and methodologies that have been deployed. While it may not be a be-all-and-end-all way to cover all aspects of doing business, we believe it can at least help business managers in understanding the ways to solve business problems within a relatively short period of time.

In the following chapters, we will explain how static Left-Right Circles can evolve into dynamic Left-Right Circles. We will also explain the various types of Left Circle and provide an understanding of their mutual relationships, as well as how to turn a Left Circle into a Right Circle. Left-Right Circles is a tool that can help you get a full picture of the business intricacies, enabling you to make good business decisions from that understanding.

Chapter 2

Guided by the Left Circle:
Using Left Circle as a Guide for
All Approaches

Starting Point in Business

This chapter explores what is "guided by the Left Circle" in a static state. Being Left Circle guided is the most important concept in business. "Customer first" is what drives our work in the first place, and everything we do should have our customers' interests and benefits in mind. Failing to do this, your business cannot be successful. Any company exists simply because it has customers. When you want your company to elevate from merely there to being successful, you need to put your best in what you do and fulfil your customers' needs in the utmost manner. This is the starting point of any business.

Other factors are crucial, such as your execution power, your people management skills, your financial astuteness and your risk management sharpness, all having a tremendous effect on the viability of your business. But if you do not take customer needs to heart, not treating customer satisfaction as your first priority (meaning not taking the "Left Circle" as your business starting point), then however you talk about the other great things you do, you are all but destined to fail.

"Guided by the Left Circle" means placing customers' needs and customers' benefits as the overarching objective of the company. This sounds easy, but it is not. The actual fact is, when a lot of companies are making important decisions, they take competitors and the competitive environment as their first concern to plan out their reactions. Over time, customers become of secondary importance to them, and everything becomes "competition guided".

Other companies put customer needs aside and focus on short-term profitability. They may switch to lower-grade raw materials and believe that customers would not notice. It would be almost impossible that it will not be found out. Such an attitude is "profit guided". Very often, we see coffee shops silently cutting back on coffee beans just to "save cost", only to be forced back to normal brewing when customers tell them that they are not satisfied with the coffee intensity.

Also common is the so-called "innovation trap". Some developers are obsessed with their sophisticated high-tech products for which they allocate large resources, significant time and tremendous energy to develop. Yet what they have ignored is to ensure these are what their target customers want, ultimately rendering all their efforts useless. Yet another phenomenon is for company leaders to act on their own personal preferences, with staff hesitant to express their reservations or opposing views, eventually taking the company down to disastrous outcomes. All these are either "product guided" or "leadership guided". Chances are they will end up failing.

Talking about being "guided by the Left Circle", many wonder why many large corporations appear to be not acting on the basis of first understanding customer needs. They seem to think they are powerful enough that customers would just follow their lead. Take Apple as an example. When a new iPhone model is rolled out, we find people seldom do requisite research to understand whether the new functions are good for them before they dash out to buy. Is this a counterexample that proves a company need not be guided by the Left Circle to be successful? What needs indeed is the new iPhone satisfying if it does follow the Left Circle guided theory?

Of course, the new iPhone model must have certain features that are improvements over the previous version. It may be better compatibility with the iOS operating system or an upgrade in efficiency and other features. But not all customers think that these are helpful to them, with some not even aware of these features. The new more complicated functions may even be confusing, so these customers groups are unlikely to see this new phone as suitable.

In fact, what is important in this Left Circle guided concept is that you thoroughly understand your Left Circle and the types of customers in there. You use that understanding as your starting point to tailor strategies and design products for your target groups. As you move into this direction, some individuals might come in to like your products while others might move out to see your products as not for them. You will be faced with a tradeoff. Even when you are guided by the Left Circle, you still have to choose which types of customers you want to target in the Left Circle, and then take steps to understand their needs.

Returning to our iPhone case, for people who buy the new model not caring about what new functions there are, they are probably the "Apple fans" who just trust the brand with some positive experience about how each new release renews the product. Yet there are others who simply feel they enjoy a special status when holding the latest iPhone set. As irrational as it may be, this is also a need to be reckoned with. Apple also chooses to put great emphasis on phone design in order to appease customers who put fashion high on their priority list.

This is what Apple chooses to do. But these elements alone are never strong enough to get everybody to buy. It has successfully convinced customers with high spending power to see those features as worthy of the price. There are strong competitors in the marketplace including Samsung, Sony and LG. In China, phone manufacturers such as Xiaomi and Huawei also roll out phones with similar functions but of significantly lower prices. As such, they have taken up a good market share in China. If Apple does not respond well to these Left Circle needs, it would raise serious questions about its ongoing sales in China.

Moving Up the Hierarchy of Needs

Generally speaking, a path that is guided by the Left Circle goes up the five levels in Maslow's Hierarchy of Needs. The Left Circle starts at the lowest level of physiological needs, including the basic essentials of food and clothing. Once these needs are satisfied, it will go up to the next level of security needs. Will there be conflicts between physiological needs and security needs? For those who remain at the very basic level, they care less about anything but just their stomachs filled. But if people are now up at the level of security needs, they may refuse to take food with large amounts of additives. They care not only about filling up but also if the food has toxic elements.

Going another level up are the social needs. In it an important element is the sense of belonging. Say, when you design a restaurant, you will consider whether the entire ambience is compatible with the taste of your Left Circle customers, and whether your brand will evoke an image that your customers will see as conforming to their own identity. If so, they will get a feeling of being home. More and more, mobile phones these days are used as a symbol of one's status and taste. Vertu was once the luxury mobile phone that had lines of precious stones surround the phone set, able to fetch some HKD100,000 for each set. That is definitely a luxury item that helps show off one's status and identity.

On the other hand, there are instances where people just buy a certain product not because it is special but because it is what most other people have. In this case, such Left Circle customers are indeed chasing a sense of social acceptance. Birds of a feather flock together. If everyone in the banking industry wears a blue suit with a red necktie, then chances are you cannot be too distinct from your peer group. This is all above satisfying physiological and security needs — a phenomenon known as "social norm".

Can products be made to satisfy the very high-level needs of esteem and self-actualization? We will skip the detailed discussion for these higher level needs to focus ourselves more on the concept. We will now look at how we can identify people's real needs noting that needs can come from all different levels.

Key to the Left Circle guided theory is the fact that every company can choose which customer groups it wishes to target and the needs it wants to satisfy. Every company can focus on specific market segments and their specific needs. As long as it can produce products that make its customers happy, it is helping to make the world a better place.

Back to our iPhone case, what different needs is the mobile phone designed to satisfy? First and foremost, it is communication. Apart from spoken communication by voice, users want other communication methods. For example, they need functions to edit texts and send out documents through their phones. Those are the very basic needs. At the same time, as more and more functions are added to the phone set, there will be a large amount of data stored, and it owes itself to security concerns as it becomes vulnerable to hacking. So, to the smartphone companies, they have to satisfactorily deliver solutions for both the communication needs and security needs, even though it may be difficult for any brand to be the best in both.

Then, above these basic functions, what are people after when they buy mobile phones? How many people are there just wanting to get the latest iPhone model to match up to their friends and be proud to be in the community of diehard "Apple fans"? But there are also people who are just happy with their everlasting old iPhones models, and those who do not even check emails with their phones. Apple's new iPhones equipped with superb email functions will not be the best for these groups. Given this, even when you are guided by the Left Circle, it is imperative that you choose your target Left Circle groups and understand their specific needs.

Conflicting Needs and Niches

As we just highlighted, needs can be conflicting at times. When products become complex and multifunctional, naturally they will be more expensive. So for some people, they may feel that they are paying a price that includes 90% of the functions that they do not use. If you need a phone that is tailor-made exactly for the 30%, 40% or 70% of the functions that you use, that tailoring may cost more and make the product even more expensive. That is why manufacturers often choose to produce standardized products for cost-effectiveness reasons, based on the concept of economies of scale.

For rice, you may think brown rice should be cheaper than white rice because it goes through one less step in the process without having to remove its outer skin. Yet it is not the case because brown rice is a need of the minority, and separate handling is required. This makes brown rice more expensive than white rice. When your need is specific, it requires special design and special processing, and the price will go up. Some people say small packaging is not environmentally friendly, but if the intended use of a toothpaste is for travel, using a large-size one can be wasteful. It takes all kinds of people to make a world. Everyone has his own specific needs. A company needs to determine the persons in its Left Circle it wants to serve, find out what their needs are, and apply its ability to come up with ways that satisfy those needs.

Take a moment to think. What you can do is limited. No company can satisfy all the needs in the market. The trick is in how you can use a targeted way to understand your Left Circle customer needs and match them with your Right Circle abilities. The matching area is Area C as described in Chapter 1. The needs that you cannot match with your abilities become Area A. The fact that Area A exists reflects a truth: you cannot satisfy all the needs in this world.

How do business managers look at the niche markets? It follows a theory of "I take what others don't". Today, you are still seeing electronic pagers used by some people. It satisfies a small group of people with specific needs, sustaining the survival of a small group of businesses supplying them. We may even have needs that cannot be supported in a business sense, but there are forces outside of the commercial world, such as governments, NGOs and social enterprises, that can cater to those needs for good reasons beyond profit motivations. Even if profit is not achievable from certain groups whose well-being deserves to be respected, they are still in the Left Circle with needs to be satisfied. Non-commercial activities are also Left Circle guided.

The Left Circle Guided Approach Takes You to Your Vision and Strategy

The key point in a Left Circle guided approach is to observe and choose your favoured customer groups to direct what you do in business. If you do not choose, it is difficult to drill down to some detailed understanding of what your target customers need. Many people are complacent, looking at the world from their own standing and believing that their products must have their own admirers. But this is an inward-looking approach guided by the Right Circle, not at all a Left Circle guided one. These people guided by the Right Circle will not actively go and satisfy any specific target group's needs, and they lose focus in a forward view about their business.

This loss of focus will lead them on to a path of no effective strategy, no vision, no objective, and no tactics. Nokia is a classic example. When the mobile phone market was in an earlier stage, the company commissioned a market research study in an attempt to understand the needs of China's market, and the result gave them a positive note. Yet Nokia believed that consumers in China had yet attained a level of affordability for widespread use of smartphones, a conclusion for which management should now be bitterly regretting. Many companies are blinded by their own success, ignoring to keep track of the Left Circle needs.

Not taking a Left Circle guided approach will stall your company's progress. More seriously, you may be going in an opposite direction to the way your Left Circle moves. You may be able to hang on for a while if you are lucky, but it will not last as we see from our Left-Right Circles theory. The fact is that your competitors will not do the same as you do as they never ignore their Left Circles.

Do you know the exact needs you should be satisfying to enable you to construct efforts towards those needs? If you simply stick to your own guns and ignore the validity of needs outside, you are simply asking trouble for yourself. In fact, many people do get themselves into trouble without realizing they should be working to satisfy other people's needs. I use the example of a student. Asked as to why he should study hard, he might say it is for making money. But in exactly what way he can make a lot of money, his answer could be "just to do my best". What exactly does it mean by doing his best? There is no specific target and no methods by which to achieve the success he wants.

You may say when you do your best, you can produce a world-beater product. And this world-beater product has the highest quality with the lowest cost and thus the lowest price, supported by the most powerful marketing campaign. But do we have such a product in this world? If you have the highest quality, why do you need the lowest price to compete? Is it that no one would buy anything that is expensive?

Sometimes a patient would ask the doctor to do more to treat his illness hoping for good effects, but usually "doing more" would come with a higher price. Yet it is common to see many who simply ask for higher cost treatment especially for their loved ones on the belief that this would be more effective. Doing extra for the patients is an approach guided by the Left Circle and not one that is just following a routine. Besides, every doctor should take steps to understand the patient through observation, listening, inquiry and examination. This practice is no doubt guided by the Left Circle.

Doctors need to look after their patients' needs, even with special needs. An ear, nose and mouth (ENT) physician cannot apply his ENT treatment methods to deal with a patient who has an ankle sprain. As a doctor, you look after your patients with their best interests in mind. If it is an ankle sprain and you are an ENT specialist, then it is far better to refer the patient to the right medical professional. When you do the referral, you are doing it for the best interests of the patient. You may have the chance to earn some fees, but those fees are not yours. The patient may just come because you are the closest doctor to him. While you may be the best ENT physician in town, you still have to take your patient's needs first in your method of treatment.

Even within the discipline of otolaryngology, there are specialty areas, such as those for traumatic disorders, genetic disorders and chronic illnesses. These specialty areas in a way belong to different Left Circles, each having its own set of needs. Some count principally on medicines as treatment while others use physiotherapy as the main correction mechanism. To the extreme, you can treat a patient by just giving him advice. That is, just to ask him to speak more softly, which can solve his problem of hoarse throat without medication. The more you understand the patient's conditions and needs, the more suitable your method can be to solve his issues.

This example of the ENT specialist demonstrates the essence of a Left Circle guided approach. You have to see the matter from your patient's angle, understand why he comes to the current condition, estimate how he wants it done, and then apply the best treatment method. A special note about an approach guided by the Left Circle is that you can never be completely sure about the needs of your customers, but you can apply an "educated guess" on what those needs are. Since you are the specialist in your field, you should have the best knowledge for your profession. Your guess has to be better than anyone else's. As well, your skills and methods should be superior, although all these will come to no avail if you do not understand who your target groups are and what exactly they need.

A Product is Not Only a Product

This whole concept has applications in all facets of life including the daily essentials of clothing, food, housing and transportation, as well as education, entertainment and even finance. Everything operates within an environment guided by the Left Circle. Why would one buy distinctly different styles of clothing from both the Uniqlo and Armani brands? Why would one own three watches when one is functionally enough? This may be out of different needs for different occasions. For instance, you would wear a special watch at your daughter's wedding, not as a show-off but a respect for the occasion. You put high value on this memorable occasion to warrant a special trip to fetch your expensive watch from the safe. In this respect, a watch is not simply a watch at the wedding.

Just another example. Where would you normally go to eat? Anywhere, perhaps. One day when your favourite teacher passes by from afar, where would you bring him for a nice meal? You would normally ask the teacher where and what he prefers, but the answer is usually any- where and anything. At this time, you would seriously think about your teacher's tastes and preferences, and remember an occasion where he took you to a certain restaurant. As you find the restaurant is still there, you decide to take your teacher to the place once again to reminisce the happy past.

Once there, you remind your teacher that both of you were there 30 years ago, bringing out all the sweet memories that he may now only hazily recall. The restaurant is not merely a restaurant but a place where you and your teacher can draw tenderness from. This specific restaurant is what you use to build the love and warmth you wish to enjoy once more with your teacher. Suddenly a thought comes to light in your teacher's mind: "I have never imagined that something I've done 30 years ago has this profound impact on my student, and I should now take comfort in all this that I've done."

Noting this, will you see things from a Left Circle perspective to appreciate the different behaviours? If you do not go deep into your Left Circle customers' minds, you are incapable of working out any good mar- keting campaigns. Why do some people still stick to the same area after several moves? Is that because this is the catchment area of a certain school that they favour? Is it related to the sentiments people hold having grown up in the area? Why do people go back to the doctor near their old home even after they have moved to another area? It may be a bit far, but is there a special feeling and certain trust that draws the patient back to the doctor? If you consider seeing a doctor a mere mechanical process to have an illness cured, then you have missed out totally on what an approach guided by the Left Circle can work for you.

Many doctors are good not only because they have a deep understand- ing on medical knowledge but more because they are very caring. Such an attitude is probably not taught in their professional training, and patients may not even expect it from their doctors. But if you are not adopting an approach guided by the Left Circle, then what use is your superb medical skills? If you act disdainfully against your patients and are unwilling to answer their questions, you have no way to understand their needs. Never mind how effective your prescriptions can be, you are unlikely to reach the level of a distinguished doctor.

As the Chinese saying goes: "A doctor should be charitable in thought and deed." A "thought" has to come before a "deed". The latter is only a technical method used to cure a disease. A caring thought has to come first, otherwise the patient will feel uncomfortable wondering if the doctor is doing all he can for his benefit. However superb the doctor's skills may be, a caring thought is essential to qualify him as top-class. How can a doctor be guided by the Left Circle? What is a doctor's objective — treating the patient or treating the disease? Treating the disease requires just the "deed"; treating the patient demands a caring "thought" to be dispensed before the deed.

A "Guided by the Left Circle" Example: To Be a Good Teacher

How do you judge what makes a good teacher? Is it one who has the requisite professional knowledge and can teach by the book? Is it good enough just to make sure the students understand the meanings of the materials taught in class? Is it important to know if the students really like the subjects? If you care only about the job of imparting knowledge, and not about raising learning interest, you are simply guided by the Right Circle. You are just following your own model when you do your job. Learning should not end with the class. How can you maintain an insatiable interest in your students so that they keep learning to new heights?

Just because you are a famous professor, you may think that it is alright for you to do it your way, not caring too much about your students' feelings, ignoring their difficulties, and just letting them find their own way to keep up with the work. But are you fulfilling your teaching objectives by helping students to satisfy their needs? Are you looking at the whole matter from your students' point of view? Remember, you are the one responsible for getting your students to the desired level, and leaving them on their own may not give them the capability to produce a thesis to the required standard. For you to do just simple one-on-one pep talks with your students, you may inspire them to a different temperament and a broader worldview. Easily your students can raise themselves to much higher levels.

Teachers can use their lives to influence other lives. This is teaching beyond techniques. Can a teacher who does not see his students be regarded as a good teacher? Students may watch his lessons via video links in the modern era, but where can they get a mutual relationship developed?

To determine whether you are a good teacher or not, it depends on your value of life and a link with your Left Circle. You ask this crucial first question: why do you want to be a teacher? If you think that your duty is just to explain the materials, your enthusiasm in teaching has probably come to a standstill. If you do have a passion towards teaching, you would want to mix with your students and conduct meaningful exchanges in intellectual and spiritual terms. All this cannot be done using a Right Circle guided approach.

As a teacher, your Left Circle can be primary, secondary, undergraduate, postgraduate or doctoral students. Each of these Left Circle constituents has its special needs. The language and teaching method you use against each type ought to be different, very much tailored to the circumstances. This approach is certainly guided by the Left Circle. On the contrary, as you talk incessantly on the stage, you may see it as a great speech. Yet if your audience has difficulties understanding what you want to convey, then you have simply used a wrong method. Hence, when speaking to a small kid, just speak in the language for the kid.

First, you need to identify your target, your Left Circle. Then, you choose the best method for your target. Yet, recognizing that there are multiple needs within one target, you may have to choose exactly which needs you want to satisfy. We have an example below to illustrate:

On one occasion, a university professor was invited to speak to some primary students. If he went for a language that only university students can understand, the primary students would all be at a complete loss. But his speech that day had drawn all the plaudits. Let us look at how this conversation went:

Professor: "Who are the people here today?"
Student: "They are the teachers."
Professor: "Anyone else?"
Student: "Parents also."
Professor: "Are they the ones who love you most?"
Student: "Yes."
Professor: "Do you think they are clever?"
Student: "Yes, they are clever."
Professor: "They love you and they are clever. Do you listen to them?"
Student: "Yes, I do."

Indeed, this conversation exemplifies what a Left Circle guided approach is.

This professor was very clear about who the target audience was in his Left Circle. It was the primary school principal and teachers who invited him. The main audience, however, was the primary students. He knew he had to consider what those very young students wanted. But he also knew there were others in the audience, namely the parents and the teachers. The conversation he conducted above with the primary students would have earned the praise from the adult audience too.

Should the professor use his usual style at the university to address the primary school audience, there would have been a big gap in understanding. Even if the adults in the audience might have appreciated the professor's deep knowledge, the whole speech would have been ill-suited for the occasion. If his speech was not made to pinpoint that specific audience group, he would just be using a Right Circle guided approach.

Pinpointing the primary students, the professor uses the simplest language to address them without causing any ambiguity. Apart from the language, the subject should also be towards the interests of primary students. In fact, even primary students have multiple needs. Some of them are very fond of the cartoon character "Doraemon" and its stories. While telling those stories may seem to have satisfied some of their needs, the issue is what can they take away from the occasion? Will that help them in any way in their growing up?

Primary students at their stage do not know all the right questions to ask. Educators have a responsibility to make an educated guess as to what the relevant issues are. In the course of growing up, their parents and teachers are the important people who will give them love and warmth and will greatly impact their future. If you can help the students to strengthen their relationships with these most precious people around them, that would be the biggest favour you can do them for their long-term benefit.

The speech would also benefit the parents and teachers as his other Left Circle constituents. When the children are asked to respect and listen to their parents and teachers, this sends a message to the latter groups telling them how important they are in the course of bringing up the children. This reinforces a sense of duty towards the children, demanding from them their best care and help.

Parents and teachers are there to ensure the children grow up happily and healthily. Parents should genuinely love their children and not use them as a way to flaunt their achievements, say in the form of their elite-school status, to their friends and neighbours. The message also asks teachers not to treat teaching as just a job, realizing that the future of their students is very much in their hands. The professor can address all his Left Circle groups through this short speech. This would not be possible if he does not have an intimate knowledge of his Left Circle.

As a side note, the professor had inadvertently thought that his speech was to be delivered to secondary students instead of primary students. He made last-minute adjustments to his approach and the speech content. Should he not be totally conversant with the Left Circle guided approach, he would not have made this event a success. The worst case would be for him to use his professor stature to address the small children. Even when the professor speaks to university students, he has to employ different styles and methods to suit the situations. The best speech is one that addresses the audience's needs directly and accurately. But to be able to do that, one has to figure out those pertinent needs and come up with the best way of delivering the message.

Prerequisites for Executing an Approach Guided by the Left Circle

We wish to give a view of the two conditions necessary for carrying out an approach guided by the Left Circle. As you have gone through the examples above, you should have an appreciation of what they are. Not able to satisfy these two prerequisites, the Left Circle guided approach will not make sense at all.

Understanding the characteristics of the Left Circle

Among the life essentials, I will now use transportation as my case to illustrate. When choosing our mode of transportation, what are the considerations from a Left Circle perspective? Are we always going for cost-effectiveness aiming to get the least cost to cover the longest distance? Not necessarily. On a rainy day, you would probably want a more convenient mode of transportation despite its higher cost. And if you want to be absolutely on time for an important meeting, the more expensive way may be your choice too. Going from A to B, the choice of which transportation mode depends on such factors as the weather, your mood, your specific need and your condition, among others.

Some people may change their needs and wants completely in just a day. For someone who is to seek the highest productivity and efficiency would definitely take the fastest way to commute. He may even want the opportunity to conduct work or business while he is on the road. He would hire a chauffeur to take him everywhere in his own private car. But on this day when he starts his retirement life, he has ample time to spare. Now he wants to take life easily and prefers to move around on foot or on public transportation. As his circumstances change, his needs change completely too, all within a day.

That is the reason why there is no one mode of transportation which can satisfy all the people. Each mode is serving some specific needs and has its own target groups. Who is the MTR metro system serving? What are the functions of the buses and trams? Why should trams exist when there are buses? Who are those that take the trams? Using the perspectives of the tram passengers, we understand that a lot would go for it because it is cheap and easy, particularly for short journeys. But some would favour the nostalgic feel from this old tram.

Even for the ubiquitous MTR metro, it does not cover all the needs. Usually people take it for long distances and use other modes for shorter ones. They do it this way either for cost reasons or because they do not want to walk up and down inside the MTR stations when they spend only a short time in the train. Even the ability to take a nap is an important consideration for some. Still others avoid taxis at all cost because they hate being disturbed by the drivers' chitchat talks. Of course, a lot of people just do not care, as long as they get to where they want easily. As different people have different needs, the people you see on the MTR, on buses, on trams and in taxis, are taking up their choices based on what they need.

If you do not consider those factors, you cannot be considered Left Circle guided. As you make your choice of the Left Circle to serve, you have to understand all the characteristics that are guiding needs. To be successful, understanding your Left Circle characteristics is a must. Without such understanding, you may have to count on luck. But luck, as we know, never lasts.

Choosing a Left Circle right for you

The second Left Circle guided prerequisite is to choose the Left Circle that is the best for your Right Circle (i.e. yourself). People in this world have all different needs, in life essentials, in education, in entertainment and in all other sectors. At the same time, there are many service providers willing to provide services of all kinds. Who do you choose to serve? Running a business, of course you would want to target those to whom you can provide the best results over and above all your competitors.

As you choose your Left Circle, you would match it with your own value system as well. You might choose a sector that is seen as "anti-trend". But that is not wrong. Nothing stops you from going against the trend, as there are people who do want something different. When everybody is going for the money in a certain sector, you might want to target some underprivileged groups for intangible rewards. For example, due to environmental concerns, you may choose to use raw materials that can decompose naturally. The cost is higher, but your contribution to the world is worth more. The whole matter may just mean a little less profit, but it goes fully compatible with your deep-seated value system.

"A man of honour knows what to do and what not to do." Profit is secondary. This is your choice. What others do is not necessarily wrong, but neither are you. All it says is this is just a choice. There are people who go to rural areas to teach. Médecins sans frontiers doctors serve in war-ravaged areas. Why do these people choose to do tough jobs and even risk their lives instead of staying in comfortable places? Whatever the reason, this is the Left Circle they choose to serve.

Yet you still have to look at whether you are up to it in your ability to serve your preferred Left Circle. If you do not have a physical (or more importantly, mental) condition that enables you to survive in war zones, you should not expose yourself to such dangers. If you think you will have altitude sickness, you should not go to the mountains but choose other areas to serve. It is not about challenging your limits. You have to be sure you have a firm ability to overcome problems in your Left Circle. What you choose should be ones that blend in nicely with your strengths. Then, this is truly an approach guided by the Left Circle.

As you make your choice, you are in fact also pushing your way forward. The Left Circle you have chosen may have more than one set of needs. Some needs are not known yet. But once Set One is satisfied, you will find more with Set Two, and this goes on. The interactive forces between the Left and Right Circles will take you to the process of a next-phase discovery.

You need to take into account your Right Circle ability. But if your starting point is just what you are doing, then it is likely that you have little idea of who you are serving. Even if you are a very large company already in a lot of sectors, chances are you do not have a focus. You are lacking a drive from your Left Circle that tells you why you are in business.

You Only Know What it is Like When You Have Been Through it

Even when the Left Circle is your guiding light, that does not mean it tells you clearly what all the requirements are. As you observe, you would know better what is obvious and what is not. Saying is one thing, doing is another. How people act gives firm clues as to what their real needs are. Their reactions to your actual services and products are the truths you are seeking.

A lot of times, the Left Circle has no way to express its needs, particularly when confronting new and innovative products. When people have no experience in a certain matter, they have no way of telling you whether they like it or not. It is said that the concept of Walkman was initiated by an American company, but they abandoned it after results from a research study told them that there was no such need in the market. The concept was later picked up by Sony, and the rest is history.

The truth was revealed by Sony after the company put the product in the market. But you may never know it for sure until you have put your hands on it. "You won't know it until you're there" refers to the situation where you can only appreciate the whole scenery when you are actually in the place. Just as you have five routes to choose from, and you have chosen Route A. You have walked it, and you know where it takes you (i.e. success or failure). But still you have no idea about Routes B, C, D and E, because you simply have not walked them.

You Can Choose Another Left Circle

We know that the Left Circle constantly moves. If your Right Circle always stays the same, you will become further and further away from the Left Circle. This is not what we want. But we can develop a different scenario in that you can actually choose another Left Circle. We can use our teaching experience as an example. Certainly, our Left-Right Circles theory can be taught to as many people as possible regardless of their knowledge base and prior experience. But it would be unsuitable to go too deep for general understanding. Alternatively, we can recruit three to five keen learners to become our top students. In this case, these advanced learners can be given more information so they can spread it to more people in ways more suitable for the individuals.

When you seek change, one way is to change your audience rather than your product. Just at this point, we have left the lecturer room and come to the desk to write up this theory. This is our choice to go after a new Left Circle who we hope will read our book. Yet another option would be to continually promote the Left Circle guided theory to new students in university each year, hoping that one day one of them would succeed in developing another breakthrough theory on top of ours. As we could develop this theory from our teaching experience, our students can be just as good going forward. Relying on them to carry the baton can be just as viable an option.

Given all this, choosing your Left Circle and doing the right things to meet the Left Circle needs is very important. You need to pay special attention to the conditions of your Left Circle. For getting the students to carry on with the Left-Right Circles theory, how well they can learn and express themselves, and how passionate they are in pursuing the matter, can have great bearing on whether our wish will come true.

We have a special group very close to us. They are the ones who would dedicate their time and energy to the study of the Left-Right Circles theory. Keeping these valuable resources is crucial, but they need to feel happy and satisfied to remain in the group. They are indeed the Left Circle of our mission. We will have to maintain some very productive relationships recognizing the individual characteristics. Say for Member A, the best communication would be through a sterner way in text, while for Members B and C, chats and casual pop-out comments are seen more suitable.

The key in all this is that you have to respect your Left Circle, acknowledge their needs, and adjust your methods to suit them. Our methods change with the times. We have now moved to Facebook and other online social media. In the past, our seminars and discussion forums were restricted to our own students, but now they are open to other people. We hope by this we will encourage even better exchanges. We continually make choices coping with the changing needs.

Next, we will be discussing the ever-changing Left Circle in Chapter 3.

Chapter 3

Dynamic Left Circle

The last chapter explains the importance of a Left Circle guided approach led by an objective to satisfy the needs therein. This chapter goes deeper into the concept and recognizes that the Left Circle will move. The Left Circle we know today may not be the same Left Circle we will see tomorrow. What's more, the Left Circle needs that we see may not be the real needs that we have to deal with. To understand what exactly has to be satisfied, we need to grasp those movements and zero in on the deeper needs of the Left Circle.

Movements of the Left Circle

The Left Circle focuses on customer needs. The Right Circle points to our abilities or competences. The Left-Right Circles theory is premised on how we use our strengths (i.e. competences) to meet the needs we want to satisfy. No one can use one strategy or a single method to satisfy the needs of all people. It is only that for a particular need, a certain company is doing better to produce results than the others in satisfying this need. This creates an intersecting area between the Left and Right Circles, called Area C. This area is where the company's competences meet the needs of its target customers, shown as the overlapping area between the Left and Right Circles in our theory.

But the situations are more complicated than a static or stationary Left Circle can cover. The first force of change comes from the fact that people are ever-changing. Physically, we will grow old, lose our energy or get hungry. Psychologically, we can turn from being happy to unhappy.

And the people around us may have new ideas and start doing things differently. For stance, when someone saw other people running during his routine commute, an idea popped up that he should get off a bit earlier and walk the rest of the journey. That triggered his thought about taking the opportunity to do some exercise. The inspiration came from watching what others do.

The other force of change is the competition. When you are working on your customer needs, there are other providers targeting the same group of customers, aiming at taking away your business. Even if you are very focused on a certain group, other companies are extending their best efforts with various strengths and abilities to try to get a larger share of the business. Say, you are very good at your service, but some of your competitors use lower price to compete, particularly targeting customers who do not need service level to be as high. Still others would target your service being a little slower than theirs so as to take business away from you.

Just for a normal week, because of different situations, it is common that you want different things for different days. Let's look at food. On day one, for example, you wish to reminisce with your high school friend what it was like during your school days and decide to eat near your old school. What you want is to muse over things in the past, and food is secondary. On day two, you treasure the opportunity to be with your son, so you do not mind what to eat but simply want your son's company as he has half an hour for you during his lunch break. So, for two days, your needs are totally different.

On day three, all you need is a good rest. As such, you take three hours not answering phone calls, grab a coffee and some biscuits, and just sit there to watch the world go by. Yet, come the next day, as the company's CEO, your responsibility is to conduct a big conference, and all you can afford is a glass of water for the whole duration. Afterwards, you go and enjoy fine dining just as you deserve it.

If you consider a restaurant as just to serve food, it is no different from seeing all things as to have to be both cheap and good. This is a simplistic view of a much more complex issue. A lot of people do not take price as the most important factor. They have a lot more factors to consider than price. For a certain meal, the decision of where to eat depends on so much more, such as your mood on the day, who you are with, and even what you do afterwards. Some restaurants choose to offer delicate food, even tailoring it to your specific taste. Yet others simply think they should standardize their methods, speed up their processes and offer very affordable prices. Their food need not be meticulously prepared, and customer would not mind as long as they can be served a satisfying quantity.

This is a very dynamic world, so much so that you can only plan your actions to deal with a level of generality. You simply cannot change your positioning within a very short time. What you can do is to estimate what sort of Left Circle customers that would be around where you are and what you offer. Say, between 12 pm and 2 pm, you try to broadly figure out who will be there and what will be purchased. Perhaps, your conclusion is that most of them will want takeaways, but a few can afford some time to sit down and have a quick meal.

For a world as dynamic as this, we cannot use a static Left Circle and a static Right Circle to be your full view of the scenario. In this chapter, you will start to learn how we extend from the basic need of, say getting the stomach filled, to other needs that can be overriding in the customer decision. Most of the time, it is the various aspects of the environment that determine whether the customer will come. Why would customers go to a certain restaurant that demands a very high price? When it is your wedding anniversary, it counts much less for the food in your stomach than all the environmental factors that give you the chance to show respect and feelings. That special occasion is to fulfil a special feel, a need that is taken as the deepened Left Circle. Only when you can hold firm a concept of deepened Left Circle can you get your Right Circle to work to the desired effect.

Surely you have some knowledge of what your ability is, in terms of your cooking skill, service level, ambience and service efficiency. Your knowledge will take you to an idea of what your key offer should be from the Right Circle. If you do not see any of your Right Circle abilities matching up to the Left Circle needs, you have no Area C, and you have to reconsider everything. If three months ago your idea was to offer outdoors leisure seating, the current plan to start constructing a new metro line would definitely upset your entire plan. While the needs for fresh air and leisure seating are still there, no one is now able to offer anything to that effect. These are simply environmental factors beyond your control. They affect you significantly though, so you have to include these broad categories in your consideration.

Changes Affect How the Left and Right Circles Interact

In a nutshell, what you have to do is to figure out the Left Circle needs you wish to target, and consider if you have the requisite abilities to satisfy those needs. In terms of competition, you have to consider how you want to position yourself *vis-à-vis* others. In terms of the environment, you have to find out its status. But one thing to remember is that this is a dynamic world, and complete change can take place just within a day.

If you are running a Chinese restaurant, your chef in charge may come into a dispute and decide to take the entire kitchen crew with him to go elsewhere. Your strength now becomes your weakness. But then this affects only the main section of the kitchen, with resources in the dim-sum section still remaining intact. Your temporary plan could be to now concentrate on offering dim-sum dishes until resources are put back.

But if you still stick to your original positioning, insisting that your name represents the most prestigious place for the finest cuisines, then your customers will not appreciate it when your kitchen cannot keep up with the standard. Your restaurant used to be one that someone happily takes his mother to for celebrating her birthday. But as he finds its quality significantly downgraded, not even able to produce the dish that his mother values so much from the memory of her wedding day, they will definitely not come back. They do not see it as being able to hold up to its name anymore.

The Left Circle has not changed in the above example. It is just that you cannot even satisfy your existing Area C. Your Right Circle has failed to do the job that your existing Left Circle expects. Your business cannot keep up.

Besides, the Left Circle never stays unchanged. Sometimes, it is just that the Left Circle wants new experiences. Other times, the environment around the Left Circle has changed. Someone might have no issue with money in the past, and he came to your restaurant to enjoy all kinds of luxurious delicacies when he was flying high. Yet after the financial crisis, he would have to scale down his lavish lifestyle even though he still treasures a taste of the past. Now as he comes, he can only afford cheaper dishes. Should your staff not recognize this change and keep on selling him luxurious dishes, he will feel dejected and avoid your place altogether.

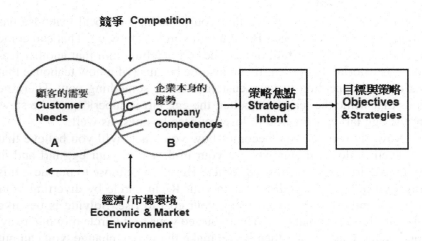

Figure 1: The Left Circle has moved left, leaving behind a smaller overlapping area.

The departure of the Left Circle as in the case above is termed "the Left Circle moving left" in our theory (Figure 1). If your Right Circle just stays in the same position while your Left Circle moves left, you are bound to lose customers because you are now unable to satisfy those customer needs in your Left Circle. This is the case of the staff above using the same manner to serve the customer without recognizing that a change has taken place.

If your Left Circle has changed but your Right Circle does not follow suit, you will see your Left Circle gradually moving away until it becomes untouchable to your Right Circle. To illustrate this situation through the diagram above, it is that the Right Circle remains the same on the right, but the Left Circle moves towards the left further and further away from you. Many companies establish themselves through a well-known product, such as the popular electronic dictionary some years ago, but as the Left Circle moves away, in this case due to the internet and smartphone, the company has lost all its appeal to the market after it fails to move with the change.

The dynamic Left Circle actually starts from a static Left Circle. In a static state, you figure out your target groups whose needs you want to satisfy. You also figure out what abilities you have to satisfy them. In that competitive environment, you establish yourself on an Area C where needs are satisfied by your abilities.

For example, the milk tea that you offer in your local teahouse has satisfied a certain customer. But the Left Circle is moving. That can come from the customer himself, or a friend of his telling him that another teahouse is offering better tea. It can also be because of a new teahouse that has opened appealing to your customer to try something new. There he finds that while the tea is not better, the egg tart is superior, and he stays for the egg tart causing you to lose your tea business as well.

Now, the whole issue becomes how you react. Will you believe that you need to do all things well, in your milk tea, in your egg tart and in your cake, to hold on to this customer? But if you choose to pursue it this way, you may dilute your power in your Right Circle by diverting your attention and possibly also causing your cost to rise. Solving issues like this requires a fine balance. When you see your Left Circle moving away, you need to change. But then if you make the wrong change, you can put yourself in peril as well.

Moving Faster Than the Left Circle: Area D in Left-Right Circles

Another concept that can be even more dynamic is that your Right Circle moves first into a certain position when you anticipate the Left Circle will move too into it. When you are the first to move into a certain position, you give your customers an impression that your service is always the best. They believe you put your customers first, knowing what they need very closely.

The dynamic Left Circle is now interpreted in relative terms — your Right Circle must move faster to the left than your Left Circle. If you do that, you prove yourself a high-quality provider. Customers cannot even tell this is their need, but once the product hits the market, they will find it the perfect one they want. The smartphone is a typical case of this potential need. Before smartphone, the old mobile phone essentially just satisfied communication needs. People had no idea about a smarter phone that can be that powerful. But once it becomes widely available, people rush to jump on the bandwagon.

If you move at the same pace as your Left Circle, the best you can do is to maintain your business. If you can move faster than your Left Circle, then you will create a situation as demonstrated in Figure 2. We talked about that in Chapter 1 — Area D and Area C are both what your Left

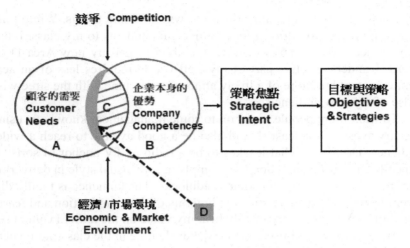

Figure 2: Emergence of Area D.

Circle needs. The difference is that Area C represents the needs that your company can satisfy now, whereas Area D has needs that are yet to be satisfied though your company is making a move towards them.

Why do we need to first move to Area D while there are still other areas in Area A? It is because Area D is closer to our abilities and it is easier to move into from Area C. To use excessive efforts to tackle other areas of needs, it can easily be all futile efforts. To choose Area D means we are being practical going for an easier task with higher probability of success.

Say, I am a Professor of Marketing, so how can I develop my Area D? What jobs can I also do close to my Right Circle that can create impact? How can I extend my teaching ability to an area where new needs can be satisfied? One area I look at is the small and medium-sized enterprise (SME) sector where business owners usually lack marketing training. Traditional university courses seldom have materials catering to their needs. What I hope is to have more people understand marketing so as to minimize mistakes in this sector.

For this, I can use my strength in teaching and speaking to conduct meetings and seminars, as well as provide management training courses. I can also use my research experience to help others do research, and convert my knowledge into books and articles. All these are good applications of my strengths. But I understand I have to take the first step out of my usual operating zone and adjust my way of doing things. While I am certain I am able to attract a lot of university students to my class, I also know I need development of a new method to get my new Area D on board. I understand this part of my Left Circle requires less of an academic content but more of a lively atmosphere in tune with the streetwise pulse of my new audience.

To want more people to get on to some management knowhow, using the airwaves to broadcast should also be a good avenue to reach a wider audience. Do I have what it takes to be a radio or TV anchor of sorts? It depends on how I want it done. If I simply use my usual style in delivering lectures, I will probably hit some roadblocks. The audience is totally different from the university students in terms of their motivation and learning ability. While people can only hear my voice on the radio, I cannot see the audience, nor can I use any visual aids. Unlike in the classroom where I can get a glimpse of my students' gestures, now I have no way of knowing their reactions.

As I move into my Area D delivering to a wider audience through a different channel, do I have to change my Right Circle? Definitely. Now that TV channels come and film my show in front of a live audience, I have to dress up a bit despite my usual habit of caring little about my appearance. I have to fit into the occasion and abandon my classroom model coming into this environment. Even references to the term "Left Circle" have to be avoided altogether — just say "customers".

As we develop new audiences, I may still come across people with sound management knowledge in my broadcast, who may raise arguments that the Left Circle includes not only customers but also colleagues. While going full force with Area D development, I simply cannot ignore my original business and positioning. This will produce a situation where I have to look after two worlds at the same time.

As you continue to develop Area D in line with the Left Circle movement, the importance of Area D will increase. It may come to a situation where Area D overtakes Area C as your mainstay. This does happen regularly in business.

Conversely, the continuous movement of the Left Circle to the left may make you redundant one day if you fail to make corresponding changes. City-dwellers today find themselves being fed too well with food rich in protein and fat. Oily, extra-sweet and salty food is now out of favour. The trend is for less meat and more vegetables, even totally vegetarian. To retain the texture that people like, some innovative businesses start offering vegetarian burgers, combining the essence of fast food, meat-like texture and vegetarian benefit. These people have gone into Area D.

Coming into this new environment where people have new demands, are you able to move your Right Circle towards these changed needs? If you take no action, your dynamic Left Circle will surely leave you behind. Once the Left Circle has left, you will have serious problems capturing it back, because loyal customers are extremely difficult to nurture.

Now the decision is that you would change. But as in the case we just discussed of a Professor of Marketing moving over to an Area D in giving speech and radio broadcast, do you think you will succeed in this move? We might say that if you do not move, you will definitely face great problems. But as you move, equally it may not be smooth sailing. It all depends on how you see the world changing and how you define the needs that you are now facing up to.

Your company will have to develop insights into the social change that affects what your target customers want. Even with those insights, you still have to search for a solid solution from the flimsy clues in order to deliver the required results. To be successful in finding a new road ahead, you have to count on good theories, keen observations and useful experience. Certainly, you need a good team with you. Your team members are the source of power that you need to stimulate you to a new level of thinking about your business.

In a dynamic world, strategic moves contain risks. But risks are reduced if you have a solid theoretical base, achieved by detailed and accurate observations and a firm grasp of how the world operates. The more relevant is your decision, the higher chance of success is your venture. This is crucial in dealing with the dynamic Left Circle. Once the dynamic Left Circle moves, your Right Circle has to move. When your move is slower, you are behind. When your move is at the same speed, you maintain what you have. When you move faster than your Left Circle, you get an advantage.

Business schools talk a lot about disruptive technologies. According to Professor Clayton M. Christensen, old technologies are constantly replaced by new technologies, such as the smartphone replacing the small camera and the personal computer replacing the typewriter. The concept of disruptive technologies provides a lot of food for thought for the Area D discussion in our Left-Right Circle studies.

To develop an Area D, you have to come up with a new way no one has done before. You will be serving a new need bringing about greater satisfaction. As time goes by, more and more customers are attracted to your new service or product, until it becomes the mainstream practice replacing the old practice. But 10 or 20 years later, you may be facing the same fate that some new ways emerge to replace yours. The world will be moving on just as it has. If you do not move, it is equivalent to totally ignorant of moves by others. It follows that you have to continually respond to the dynamic Left Circle and find your Area D.

We would reiterate what Area D means. Area D is part of your Left Circle but currently does not overlap with your Right Circle. But it is very close to your Area C. The fact that it is in the Left Circle means it is part of the needs that can be served. You have to move towards this area before your Left Circle moves away. When you make the move, be sure you have capabilities that enable you to satisfy those needs. Otherwise, you have to strengthen your Right Circle with added capabilities.

There are all sorts of ways to strengthen your Right Circle, including new technologies and new ideas such as eliminating items that become obstacles to improvements. An example is the displacement of physical shops and use of cash by online shops and electronic payments. The retail industry is undergoing a transformation that utilizes the internet to expand sales networks covering the whole world. Paperless transaction and electronic payment form part of the integrated process by which customers can purchase products without leaving their homes. Companies, big and small, are now riding on this trend to expand their sales networks, leaving behind those who do nothing.

The Right Circle also needs to eliminate unneeded items. There are outdated items called "Dogs" in the BCG (Boston Consulting Group) Matrix that can be consigned to the past (Figure 3). Hopefully, your

Figure 3:   Boston Matrix.

company has "Cash Cows" that generate cash for now, but it may be the "Question Marks" that provide the answers for your future. The Question Marks are indeed your Area D. When your Question Marks firmly demonstrate their potentials, they will move on to become the "Stars". But as time goes by and your Left Circle moves on, the Stars may in turn become your Cash Cows and eventually the Dogs when the entire Left Circle moves away. As the world keeps changing, we will see everything come nicely into this pattern.

Changes do not have to be many. Fewer changes can bring more refinement. In fact, simplification can be a good change. Customers can be looking for simpler things without being overwhelmed by too many variations. Things do not have to be fancy. A lot of times, simplicity is king. Simplification in fact can be your Area D. Your strength is simplicity. You can become an expert in minimalism. So you can move into this new position and enjoy the first mover advantage, and you establish a reputation based on this idea.

World-famous IKEA started on an idea of minimalism. Its furniture has an uncomplicated design and is manufactured with the aim of letting customers self-assemble. Its production works on the concept of standardization and economies of scale. This significantly lowers the cost of production and transportation. This very concept enables it to develop into the multinational giant that we know today.

Left-Right Circles and Innovations

Innovation, by definition, is change. How do we innovate? From the Left-Right Circles perspective, innovation is to think of a new way to satisfy the Left Circle needs, which may include needs that no one has thought of before. Innovation also involves a new method or technology, meaning that you have a new Right Circle to help resolve existing problems in the Left Circle, or future problems in the Left Circle. In the past, customers did not use your product, but after your innovation, they now do. An example is that you introduce a low-cost version of your service for customers who previously could not afford it.

Is IDD call back service an innovation? From a service point of view, the quality of the voice signal is about 20% weaker, but its cost is about 95% lower. What problems does it solve? A lot of people wish to use IDD service for business or for connecting with overseas friends and relatives, but they consider the normal IDD call rates too high. That is an existing problem. Now, the new service available is much cheaper than before, and these people will see it as very useful.

For example, many seniors and retirees had great issues with the $12/minute IDD rate for calls to North America to connect with their loved ones who have moved there. Now, the cost is down to $0.12/minute and it gives them peace of mind to enjoy quality time with their overseas family members. The new call back service gives them tremendous warmth and hope that they otherwise cannot enjoy. This is something they have not thought of before. For people who are running business, the service enables them to call their customers overseas from say, 4 times a week to 14 times now, helping them tremendously in their business. There was no such offer in the past, but now it has attracted customers who did not exist before. This is an innovation that has brought good results for all.

As good as it is, innovation is not for self-appreciation or self-gratification. An innovative practice has to be able to solve some problems in society regardless of technology. The problems solved are those unserved needs in the Left Circle. If you can draw people who did not use the service to now use it, this is regarded as innovation in the Left-Right Circles context. Some new practices are often branded "innovative" when very high skills are introduced, but they may simply have no practical use at all. Consider Uber, Facebook and Google, are these products that are rolled out on the back of very difficult skills and high technology? Not necessarily. They are innovations just because they solve a lot of problems in society.

Dynamic Left Circle's Driving Force

What do you think is the main driving force for the Left Circle to move left? Self-initiative? Social norm? Herd mentality? Economic policies? Technology progress? Commercial promotions?

The biggest factor behind the Left Circle move is "self-initiative". Customers have insatiable demands for improved products. Seeking improvements is a basic human nature. "Improvements" does not mean customers want more of the same thing or a better version of the product. They want a better optimized whole product considering all aspects. Such demands are initiated by the customers themselves.

The next biggest factor is competition. Even if you are just as good, there are bound to be competitors who are upping their game. The Left Circle is avoidably moved by these offers.

Following competition, we can name technology and environment as the next two factors. These two factors together brought us the internet which, as we know, has changed the world. Other than that, the steam engine, electricity and electric light were also breakthrough technologies that allowed us to do things deemed impossible prior. But a point to note is: Should technology mean that there should be more things, possibly more expensive items and more intensive use of our earth's resources? We will talk about that later.

People consider that we have to always move with technology. But we should also be concerned about whether technological development can strike a balance with our inner needs and needs of the society.

The Left Circle Theory Deepened

Assuming I have capital and other support now, in which area should I invest my resources? In people's livelihood? In future education? In the natural environment? Or in upgrading technology? Many people believe that improved technology must bring life advancement to people, but people's material desire may also grow with technology. If the Left Circle makes demands that are over the top, do we still have to satisfy them?

Not at all. Not all Left Circle needs are worthy to be satisfied. We need to take a view as to whether such things the Left Circle wants are healthy and proper. We need to see if certain demands are only for satisfying self-gratification and will cause harm to the society at large. If you are an IT expert capable of building websites, and you are faced with requests for porn websites, would you do it considering the negative effects it would have against women, youngsters and all sectors in society? Those other stakeholders are also part of your Left Circle. When you weigh up your Left Circle needs, customers are not the only constituent you need to be concerned with though they are definitely important.

Say, I am a teacher. My students are my key Left Circle, and my duty is to help them learn. Do I have to satisfy all that they ask for? I have to see if their demands are within the objective of learning. If students demand that their assignment be cancelled, and I see the exercise helps them greatly in understanding, I would likely not abide by their wish after balancing the pros and cons. I would probably also turn down requests for no class, no reading or easier exams, etc. In my Left Circle, it also contains needs of the students' parents and their future employers as well.

Of course, we have to regularly reflect. If the exams are really too difficult for the students, will it defeat the whole purpose of learning? It does appear so. What is the purpose of exams? Is it a way to stimulate learning or just a mechanism to grade and classify students? All these are judgement issues about the real needs of all those we serve in our Left Circle.

As we mentioned earlier, among all the factors affecting our Left Circle, the biggest force is the Left Circle itself initiating demands. Then, it is the competitors, the environment and the technology that also have influences. The same is true with education. If we are backed by an excellent education culture, our jobs are a lot easier. Once that culture deteriorates or collapses, educators have to be extra careful in making sure that their work is exactly towards the real purpose. The external environment may lead to undue demands for the educators, who would then have to weigh up if these demands are working for the real purpose. Ultimately, we have to trace back to the very basic reason why we are doing what we do.

Ordinarily people see Left-Right Circles as a drive for higher efficiency, more sales or increased income. We need to go beyond this level of understanding and dig deeper into the Left Circle meanings. Many a time, the Left Circle demands are out of a rush from the herd mentality. But can this bring benefits to all by following the herd's lead? Will the herd take us to heaven or hell? We are not saying that the herd leader has ill-intentions, but we have to make judgement about whether such is a demand that has a sole purpose for popularity. When we go against the move, we may feel we are further away from the Left Circle. But we may be led into danger zones by following its lead.

Under this situation, we should use the Left-Right Circles theory to find out the real needs of the Left Circle. You may now realize that the demands are not pointing to the real Left Circle needs. The simple way of just following the herd is not the best. What you need now is to ponder over a new way of going forward. This requires more innovativeness, a greater sense of mission, more vigorous enthusiasm, plus a significant amount of time to work to a better result.

Consider this example. Government policies are what lead the public into a certain direction. It will definitely affect the Left Circle, possibly in a very far-reaching way. But if you see that the policies are not the best for society, likely to lead your Left Circle to go astray, what are your options then? If possible, you can choose one of the following to push your agenda: (1) join the government and change it from within, (2) put yourself as a candidate for the election of legislators or district councillors, (3) be a commentator on newspapers and other media, and (4) do lobbying towards governments officials and legislators.

The Link between Advertising and the Left Circle

Does advertising influence the movement of the Left Circle? Competitors' advertisements will have an effect on our Left Circle moving away. Our own advertisements are a marketing consideration, aiming at telling customers what we are good at, firming up our positioning in our Area C. When Area D appears, advertising can also tell customers what problems our Area D can help to solve. Essentially, advertising is not used to satisfy customer needs, and companies do not necessarily have to use advertising. The most important thing is to have a way to satisfy the Left Circle needs. Companies need to first construct their Area C. They only use advertising to explain how their solutions can solve the customers' problems.

To put it more succinctly, we use advertising to remind our Left Circle how our product can help them satisfy their needs. This is not to change what the customers in the Left Circle need, but to invoke customers to discover their inherent needs. No one can change what the customers inherently need. Customers may have needs that are not apparent (even to themselves), but they are already there.

For example, with all the white shirts that someone has, he needs some coloured or patterned shirts for casual occasions during holidays or for mingling with friends. Those white shirts for work are not suitable. This is out of a consideration that he needs to blend in during social occasions and to also display a certain character of his own. He finds he does not cut an energetic figure in front of others, so he has to borrow some colours from his outfit. As he puts his mind to this issue, he also makes association with a thought of which provider offering the best product. This is the time when advertising comes in. The messages that advertisers put out will help him understand the products that they are offering hoping that he will make a choice in their favour.

Can advertising create needs? We would say no. Say, I do not need a new mobile phone. Would I suddenly need a new phone after watching a certain advertisement? Instead of the advertisement creating a new need in me, I would consider it as having stimulated a desire from my inherent need. I may already have a need for a mobile phone to help me express who I am. Now that I find myself able to afford one, I would look up all the characteristics of the various brands through their advertisements to see which one fits me the most. That advertisement just prompts me to see a certain phone as the right one. I will buy, but is it that the advertisement changes what I need?

Fundamentally, needs are not created by the providers. Companies assess what needs are there and prompt them out by their offerings. What they can change is the way the Left Circle chooses to satisfy those needs. As in the example above, advertising has not changed my inherent need to "express myself" (need). But it has created a desire for that specific mobile phone (want). The advertisement tells me that this specific phone can satisfy my need. If I do not see "expressing myself" as an important aspect in my life, I will not be swayed by any advertising to that effect.

But to satisfy that need of "expressing myself", I do not have to buy a mobile phone. I can equally satisfy the same need by purchasing a new car, going to a fine-dining restaurant, or becoming a world-record holder. As long as a person feels a certain thing can help him fulfil his need, he will be stimulated by the advertisement to create a "want" for the thing that is advertised. He buys, because he already has that need, so he can be prompted by that message.

Needs Are Just a Few, but Wants Are Too Many

Talking about need and want, in Buddhism terms, there is a saying: "We only need a few things, but we want many things." These words have multiple meanings from different angles. As explained above, even for the same need, there are multiple ways to satisfy it. That leads to the many wants that we have. The more pertinent meaning is found in the phrase "needs are just a few, but wants are too many". To deal with a certain need, we have many conditions to satisfy. In fact, our physiological needs are very basic and not too many. But moving up to the higher-level needs, such as social needs, it will not be the same story.

For a temple abbot, he needs very few things to practise *dharma*. But if he wishes to preach Buddhism, the things he has to consider become a lot more. Firstly, he has to consider the time, location and method by which the Buddhist principles are preached. Secondly, he has also to look at the attitude of those who come and what he does to correspond. To share his thoughts and doctrines, naturally he has to think about his objects, i.e. his Left Circle targets who have needs and wants. To want to meet a certain need, he has many wants to sort through. This is what "needs are just a few, but wants are too many" is pointing at.

But we also have to recognize that many people are just focused on wants, amounting to thoughtless pursuits. Often, these wants do not point even to a need. This is the third inference of "we only need a few things, but we want too many things". For example, some youngsters just want to stay in their rooms spending the whole time on electronic games. These are excessive wants that lead to many problems such as learning tardiness and family disharmony. In addition, a person ought to have different missions in life to carry at various stages. But some people are found to be just after wealth all the time. They do so just for the sake of wanting to be richer, without reference to any of their basic needs. These people have got their priorities all wrong, simply giving up the forest for the trees.

We mentioned earlier that we have to make judgement about whether the Left Circle demands are proper and reasonable. We have to see if those demands are pointing to some needs. Then, we will formulate a way to have those needs satisfied. This is irrespective of whether the Left Circle is making such needs and demands explicit.

Needs that are further away from your personal needs tend to be more forgotten. We work hard not only to satisfy our own needs but also to look after our family, our society and our country. Further, do we have obligations towards our earth and the natural environment? Do you see your responsibility towards protecting the environment so that you can live a more natural lifestyle? The answer is an affirmative yes. Indeed, the issue is not just about you looking after the environment but also about you benefiting from living in a better environment. You and the nature are inseparable.

If you accept your inseparability with the nature, you have to wonder what the nature needs. The needs are indeed plenty. Many people are destroying the nature, killing many precious elements, and doing many wrong things in that respect. For instance, in conferences, each of us is given a bottle of water, but the plastic bottle requires more than 200 years to break down. More ironic is that this conference is held for the protection of the environment. That is ignorance of the basic needs.

Do we have to protect our precious hands, legs, brain and our overall health condition? Of course, we do. Extending it to our environment, do we have to respect the nature and take measures to protect it? If we have only money in our mind and ignore all needs going towards the environment, over time we will find money is all that we have left, and nothing else.

The things we do on a day-to-day basis may not bear a good connection with what we actually need. We do that without being aware of what we need. We just do what everybody is doing, as we do not want to be seen as lagging behind, even more so for wanting to be leading the pack. Well, you do not have to live a life just like others. Say, you are now a community leader, and you may now define your role as to take everybody back to a simpler world, based upon mutual love and respect, by removing barriers, class or distances between people. You will encourage people to work in partnership with their neighbours, their communities and the world at large.

If we recognize that harmony between people and harmony between human beings and the environment are needs that we have to serve, we can take it as our Left Circle. There is plenty of room for development, and our responsibility is heavy. To satisfy these deeper needs of the Left Circle, we have to advise people to see lighter the importance of quantity. We have to ask people to care less about the size of their homes, the number of cars that they have and the balances in their bank accounts. We need to ask ourselves if lives of others have become better because of us? Especially the lower tiers of our society, can we look after their needs while providing business opportunities for enterprises with a social orientation?

Conversely, you may find yourself a person who has made life difficult for others. You may have pressed your suppliers to the extreme, sought advantage at the expense of others, gone for power and status, and disadvantaged the disadvantaged. You need now to reflect on what you do and aim at a win–win environment for all. Will you maintain a healthy supplier chain? Will you forge mutually beneficial long-term partnerships? Will you forget about short-term gains and focus on the long term? Short-term people have only short-term profits to show for, but you are far better in the long term and achieve far more meaningful outcomes through your endeavours.

Do we have to single-mindedly keep rolling out new products to satisfy the Left Circle? In deepened Left Circle areas such as improving society, promoting humanity, contributing to communities, and forging harmony with nature, we have plenty of room for development. The pursuit of the largest wealth and profit may not be our best way forward. Consider this: no matter how much you earn, it is said you need no more than 3% of your accumulated wealth to look after yourself, and the rest 97% is saved. What are the best uses for these savings? Do you share more with your employees? Or for the benefit of the communities? Or as charitable donations? Or for setting up social organizations? Or to give back to your customers? Whatever way, it is best that the fruits of the labour are shared with more people.

Understanding this deepened Left Circle will give us a sense of mission and positive resoluteness. It encourages us to make contributions to the world. We on our part should promote this idea to the wider society for overall good.

Chapter 4

Identifying New Needs and New Customers

Three Levels of Left Circle: Old Needs of Left Circle, New Needs of Left Circle, New Left Circle

In this chapter, we will use a few real-life examples to explain how to put the Left-Right Circles model to work as characterized by their different levels. To use the Left Circle guided approach for real-life applications, the first question is: What are the needs in the Left Circle that have to be satisfied? Service providers know that customers use their services because they are able to satisfy their needs. These needs are existing ones with some that can be clearly spelled out and others that can yet be delineated. Let us call this segment of existing needs the "Old Left Circle" or "old needs of the Left Circle".

Case 1: Taxis

When we use taxi service to travel from point A to point B, what we expect to have are reasonably priced, on-time, safe and comfortable services. These are basic demands we have on taxis. Can we get those services? If the driver is unfamiliar with the route, or deliberately takes a longer route, he fails to deliver the expected service. Then, we may have problems with the driver's attitude. If we see he has multiple phones placed on his dashboard, as if he is working from his office to distribute orders, or turns up the radio volume to high, or talks loudly and cheerily with his friends through the radio frequency, customers will be weary of their safety and feel disturbed. Needs are not satisfied with this level of service. The very basic of the Left-Right Circles theory is to satisfy the old needs of the Left Circle.

Then, when old needs of the Left Circle are satisfied, will we come upon new needs or needs that we are unaware of? In the case of taxis, there are indeed instances where the driver does deliver services and satisfy other needs exceeding the customer's expectation. Say, when a certain driver drives very safely and exercises extreme care with small children travelling, their mothers will have complete peace of mind. Another driver understands that the passenger is worried about being late, and recommends another route that can beat the traffic, even though he also informs that there can be higher fares involved.

Drivers can show their professionalism by respecting the passengers' preferences, such as a quiet cabin free of noises from the radio or no attempts by the driver to conduct chitchat conversations. Some passengers do not mind some exchanges *en route*, but the driver has to understand the situation and behave appropriately guided by the passenger's preference. Should this level of service be delivered, the customers will certainly feel that their expectations have been exceeded.

Quoting a very satisfied customer: "I once came across a driver with whom I could conduct a good conversation while in the car. We touched upon our health issues and he recommended a Chinese herbalist to me. This was out of my expectation." Another person has a similar experience, through which he found trust towards the driver. He took the driver's contact, and now he calls him every time he needs a taxi. Once someone has received extraordinary service, he will expect it every time. This will become the new need.

Continuing with our taxi examples, we will explain the third level, the new Left Circle, representing new customers who did not take taxis before. New Left Circles should appear in all sectors. If a certain sector sees itself incapable of getting new customers, this sector is running into deep trouble. How do we see the future of the taxi business? The way to judge is possibly by seeing if this sector can continuously attract new customers.

Which non-users of taxis would now start to use the service? Perhaps, those who are under time pressure or those who want to beat the bad weather. But these are sporadic environmental factors not good enough to be taken as systematically strong reasons to get new customers to form a new Left Circle. How can a new Left Circle be formed? This is the third level of Left Circle we need now to delve into.

Let us first reiterate the structure. Level 1 is about old needs of the old Left Circle. Level 2 is about new needs of the old Left Circle. Level 3 is about the new Left Circle, which points to people who were not part of the group of existing customers but have now been attracted into this group. Using the concept we just talked about, being a service provider, we first have to ensure our existing customers are happy about our service — their very basic old needs. If this is the case, our first step is done.

Next, we have to see if we can do more to satisfy more customer needs that exist. Whether we call these the new needs or not, it is only a matter of semantics which does not change the nature. They are in fact needs that customers already have, only that we have not prompted them out previously. We are now taking steps to satisfy these new needs, or in other words, potential needs, of the old Left Circle. "New needs" is a term we use here, and we need not care too much about if they are indeed newly created needs.

A further step is to look at if there are new customers joining the Left Circle. If we find no customers joining, that means our business model is outdated, pointing to a decline. Can we rescue our old business at this time? Among all the theories, management guru Peter Drucker told us we cannot avoid a corpse from getting decayed. We may be wasting our time. What is better is to conceive new ways or a new model of doing things. From economic theories, we know our wants are boundless. We always look for better things. This pushes our world to keep on improving. This is the reason why our Right Circle should now find a new way out.

Case 2: Securities Firms

We now move from taking taxis to buying stocks and securities. How did we buy stocks some 30 or 40 years ago? Mostly, we entrusted our stock-brokers. Why did we trust someone with our money? Likely because it was someone recommended by opinion leaders, or a person we had known for long, or a service provider our friends considered reputable after using his service, or simply because the firm he worked for was carrying a good name.

At that time, one of the main roles that brokers had was to answer clients' queries. A client would call to express his investment interests, giving out his investment expectation, and the stockbroker would assess his risk tolerance profile and adjust the expectation accordingly. It is impossible to have both low risk and high return, so some adjustment was necessary from the professional point of view.

Normally clients were not as knowledgeable and would count on the broker to make recommendations. The broker would recommend either more stable industries targeting large dividend payouts or more progressive industries for higher price prospects, possibly also with a portfolio mix. After considering the industries, it would come down to which companies' stocks to invest in. Following that, it would be to set out the time to buy and what return to target before divesting the stocks.

The client had to hold a very high level of trust towards the broker, because obviously there was no way he could monitor every move by the broker on his behalf. Apart from that, the broker had to regularly provide all sorts of information to the client, backed by his knowledge in global economic trends and events that affected those trends. The broker had to be a highly qualified person. These are what the stockbroker had to do to satisfy the old needs of his Left Circle.

As the world moves on, clients now would reconsider if they should rely totally on the brokers. Even if you do not have all the relevant skills and knowledge, you can look up a lot useful information now from online sources. There are a good number of investment vehicles other than stocks that you can invest in. What you are looking for are financial gains. Whether it is from stocks, futures, unit trusts or foreign exchange, it does not really matter.

These new investment vehicles may go beyond the broker's realm of knowledge, so it is unlikely that he will recommend something beyond his knowledge. In this respect, would you still trust him to do all the investment work on your behalf? Equipped with the new information, you now have new considerations and thus new needs. Strictly speaking, those are not new needs of yours. They were part of what you were looking for in financial planning, only that now you find a new way to make those objectives real.

As a broker, how can you avoid losing customers? While you showed competence in handling your clients' old needs, they may still lose trust in you if you come short in meeting their new needs. You wonder what you can do to meet their needs. This is the time you have to change. Perhaps you should now get yourself some competence in using online information, or upgrade yourself to become a specialist in a certain product category. As your Left Circle changes, you have to change too. The Left Circle is moving to some new expectations and new modes of operation, can you and your company match up to these new demands? Only if you can rightly remodel yourself would you be able to meet those new needs of the Left Circle.

It is getting more difficult as we come into the third level of the Left Circle. How will this whole thing move? If people want more reliability, they would choose the banks. Previously most banks did not offer investment services. All they did was having you open your saving and current accounts. That left space for the brokerage firms. The competitive environment is all changed now. Just on the issue of reliability, brokerage firms cannot match the banks. Online stock buying and selling is very popular now. The whole process amounts almost to just a press of the button, with prices preset. In both cost and convenience terms, the brokerage firms are way behind.

Now you are losing your Left Circle. How can it be replaced? What do you tell your customers you can do now? Do you have some specialty services that you can provide? With new skills and knowledge, you may attract more adventurous investors into the category of derivatives. Perhaps you can also specialize in Chinese real estate stocks, developing yourself as an expert in this category. These are unreachable territories by the banks who only provide more general services and are restricted in active solicitation. Now, you should target this new level to nurture new customers. You will get new business if your customers value your expert advice.

As the old investors draw closer to their retirement, your new Left Circle should be the younger clients. How do younger people manage their finance these days? They may not buy stocks, but instead buy bonds or properties. Perhaps some young ones may just spend, seeing their future is uncertain, so they might as well just count on the government to provide them with social security. People just spending can be your biggest competitive force, taking away the money people might otherwise invest. It will be difficult for you if you let it happen.

Given this, you need to think. How can you expand your client base with new investors? Some investment houses are already working with universities to organize investment seminars for youngsters. On the one hand, it will work to enrich people's knowledge on securities and investments, while on the other hand, it can be an avenue with which to source new customers. The link with universities may source for companies' new customers who may stay with them for a lifetime. As a securities firm, you have to look for new setup and a new model. A securities firm may not be just a securities firm in the future but a place where people come to get total financial advices.

Let me summarize this whole scenario of securities firms. Why did your customers use your service at the beginning? On what basis were you able to get your firm up and running? It was because there was not much choice at the time, and you were able to provide valuable advices to your clients, so they were happy to entrust you with their stock transactions. With those services, you were able to satisfy their needs.

But as time goes by, given there is competition, customers may start to have doubt about your reliability and adequacy in terms of your professional capability, and you start to lose customers. You now need new customers to replace the old ones, otherwise you will run into trouble. You may complain that things are getting harder and harder, but that is a given. The fact is the Left Circle will almost always move left. If your Right Circle does not move, you are working against the tide and this will get you behind more and more. Many competitors will encroach upon your old Left Circle, and all that you can do now is to develop a new Left Circle.

In delineating the three levels of old needs of the old Left Circle, new needs of the old Left Circle and the new Left Circle, the first thing to do is to evaluate whether your business is indeed going up, staying stagnant or going down. You will have to craft out a response relative to which of the three levels of needs you should now be working towards. Referring back to our concept of being guided by the Left Circle, the golden rule is that if you do not move, you are doomed to fail. Yet, even if you move, it also depends on how you move. If wrong, it may also put your company in jeopardy.

Case 3: Medical Clinics

We will talk about medical service in this case. Why do people go and see a doctor? Of course, when you are sick, you need a doctor. Some parents care about their children so much that they send them to the doctor even when they only have slight discomfort. Apart from satisfying these old needs, what other things can a doctor do to be more effective?

Patients know what discipline a doctor is specialized in. For a dermatologist, the patient would only go there if he has skin problems. When he was there, he found the doctor was very kind and willing to talk about other non-skin-related health issues with him. The doctor even had observations that were not apparent to him. Do you think the patient would like him and regard him highly? Of course, he would. This is because the doctor treats him as a person, instead of just trying to treat his sickness.

"I am not treating the eye. I am treating the person with eye diseases," well said by Dr. Dennis Lam, a highly regarded ophthalmologist in Hong Kong. This caring attitude can be taken as the way patients' new needs are satisfied. Patients do not only expect doctors to treat their disease but also expect them to care about their health. Doctors need to think this over and take it up as if it is a new service to be provided.

No doubt, more healthy people means less need for service from the doctor. This seems to have contradictions with clinic services. Some doctors may even say, "If everybody gets a flu vaccination, who will come to see me?" But this is a Right Circle guided approach. These doctors may be able to satisfy the old needs of the patients, but once the patients know they have new needs, they will not come to them.

Do medical services face competition? Consider outpatient services. Hospital emergency rooms (ER) do compete with private clinics. Only because waiting time at public hospitals is long and the location is inconvenient that patients come to private clinics. In terms of reliability, how do you as a clinic doctor compete with hospital services? Are doctors in public hospitals more experienced? Are private hospitals better for specialized treatments? Doctors are in competition with various service providers for patients. The choice is with the patients depending on the aspects of service they see as important to them.

Some wealthy people still go to public hospitals preferring the wider scope of experience that their doctors have. These doctors see numerous patients in a day and must have dealt with a wide multitude of different diseases. A certain famous private doctor, on the other hand, may not have come across a particular type of illness during the past three months. But this doctor, while reputable for his superb skills, is also more attentive to patients. This sort of jockeying for positive perception is how competition takes place for the old Left Circle.

So much so for the old Left Circle, how can doctors get to a new Left Circle? For example, doctors can serve people who are more health conscious, such as by performing health check-ups for them. Latent diseases may be uncovered from regular examinations. Say, a certain customer thinks he has high cholesterol, so he comes for a check-up.

With these service offerings, the doctor is now moving towards a new Left Circle.

Doctors can also move beyond disease treatment to dealing with sub-healthy state and disease prevention. They may even get out of their clinics to get engaged in other health-related undertakings. Can doctors come to give speeches and general advices? Carrying a mission towards public health, a doctor will not feel happy seeing big crowds in front of the hospitals. Knowing full well the importance of medical practitioners in society, a doctor may volunteer to give advices on illness prevention. His sense of mission for public good can take him to a new Left Circle.

Today, people's awareness of health issues has increased significantly. Many are serious about what to eat and what not to eat, what to do and what not to do. They have good knowledge of applying self-help when certain symptoms appear. They also know the time for medical assistance when other symptoms are visible.

Now, we believe you start to realize that there can be many new Left Circles coming around. Doctors are no longer just doctors, and clinics are no longer just clinics. The ultimate need of the customer is health. That is why doctors can move from disease treatment to illness prevention, to health awareness promotion, and probably to propagation of the idea about integrating the mind and the body.

The setting today shows there are many unfinished businesses. To finish these unfinished businesses, we have to reset the setting. We can quickly discover a new setting from working through our Left-Right Circles theory. The duck knows the water first. If you are the first to grasp the Left Circle needs, you can get yourself up quickly to retain your old Left Circle and draw new Left Circles in. You can serve the wider community. This again shows the importance of an approach guided by the Left Circle.

Case 4: Libraries

The next case is a facility familiar to all of us — the library. All along, the library has been the place for knowledge. The amount of information and knowledge we can get from classroom is limited. The library arranges information sources into categories and sections, letting people do the browsing conveniently. Sometimes someone would just go straight to the section of his interest to check for new additions, or just to find the book his teacher mentions in class. The book may be in its third or fifth edition, and he may be interested in knowing the difference. If he finds the book interesting, he may borrow it and take it home.

To do research, there needs to be a lot of information gathering. If the search is not wide enough, the study will not be as deep and as extensive. A common habit is to go through the entire library, checking out all the shelves. Some situations do happen in the library. When you are heading to Shelve #3, you pass by Shelves #1 and #2. You get a glimpse of the materials there and spot a good one, and you stop to have a read. A lot of new knowledge and theories are founded in such a way. When you are on business strategies, you read a book by a certain author. Now you find a book on leadership by the same author, and you read it too. The more common cases are that you just need some leisure reading to pass the time, and the book is there to help you relieve stress and pressure.

For libraries, gathering information and acquiring knowledge are the old needs of the Left Circle. Besides, when you are in a library, you find people quietly and intensely reading and studying, and it forms an atmosphere that induces you into the same learning mode. Studying can be boring. But every time when you want to leave the library, you see your good mate still there completely absorbed. He now becomes your guiding light and teacher, role-modelling how not to give up. You simply want to stay in such a clean and peaceful environment.

Libraries gather birds of the same feather, putting them together as a flock. At the same time, librarians will turn into your friends after seeing you so often, which will make the place even more appealing to you. All these are things that were not thought about at first but got satisfied, and they are the new needs of the Left Circle.

While the Left Circle is satisfied, what kind of a world the library has to face up to now that the internet has changed almost everything? Do people still go to the library when there are powerful search engines online? Perhaps pressing a certain button is all that it needs to get all the related publications in front of you using some key words. Information search is now much easier and possibly also much broader. What can the library do to draw in a new Left Circle?

Recently some social groups organized seminars and exhibitions in libraries. This utilizes the available space for other uses than placing books. In a sense, a library is no longer a library. Our colleagues had used the Hong Kong Central Library as the venue for a Chinese music concert. Why did they choose the library? It is more to go with the common thread linking the library with their activities in the contexts of culture, knowledge and traditional values. The library is best suited to expanding into arenas of that sort.

Now cafés are common in bookstores. Coffee culture is popular in our contemporary life. If those coming for the coffee are already regular visitors to the bookstore, they are taken as the new needs of the old Left Circle. But if these visitors come for the coffee first, taking the opportunity to also do reading, then this is a new Left Circle.

Perhaps libraries can also jump on to the O2O (online-to-offline) marketing model. This will allow people to search online and receive services in the physical library environment offline. Should you make everything online, it will lose all essences of a library — the bookish feel inside and the random chances of stumbling into something useful. As well, you will lose all opportunities of person-to-person connection.

Going further, what the world is going to be like in 10 or 20 years' time is a mystery to us at this point. Libraries can be further and further from what it was like in our childhood memories. But the world will never stop, and if only the library remains the same, then we know there is a serious problem. The Left Circle will change no matter what. When the old needs are satisfied, new needs will come along. When the old Left Circle moves away, a new Left Circle will have to come to take its place. If libraries cannot get any new Left Circles, then it will definitely spell the end of such a concept.

Yet, libraries are inherently restricted by location and design. They cannot change just as they would like. Even when there are new needs, their hands are tied in a way to give satisfactory results. We can foresee some difficulties in the future in terms of development. After all, use of the space for other activities is a new way, but is this exactly what the libraries are for? Developments have to go in line with the visions and purposes. Certainly, we cannot just work on rock solid rules and have to realize that libraries cannot escape being Left Circle guided. A rethink is needed as to the whole concept.

Case 5: Business Education

Now, we will switch to business education. What should this sector do? Say, a child says he wants to study business management when he goes to university, and he will be met with two schools of thought.

One school will say that the child has demonstrated expertise in specialized areas, and he should go for other majors. Since he has joined some non-profit organizations such as the Red Cross, he should go for sociology, or social work. The premise here is that education should go with personal interests, and all needs to aim at fulfilling personal aspirations.

The other school of thought will say that he should study business management. He can find jobs easily in a commercial city like Hong Kong. This school believes that education is to serve the purpose of getting a good job, and interests can be set aside until he is well-settled in his career. So, for now, we will treat jobs as the old needs of the Left Circle for business education.

However, is the purpose for studying business management just to land a good job? Is every graduate trained to handle business with one model answer? Of course not. In fact, everyone's worldview is a result of his combined learning throughout primary school, secondary school and university, and perhaps even kindergarten, plus all the subtle influences from the people around him, including his good friends, teacher and mentor. All these influences help to build his perspectives.

Do you see all things from a money point of view? To put money first and be super-driven by personal interests, you will not get your subordinates to respect you. People will not like you. Because of you, your wife is ashamed to tell others what you do, and your children do not hold their heads up high. Is money everything?

Now, should teachers also talk about social responsibility and social contributions? Students may start with no such thoughts, but could these already be their own longing deep down? As educators integrate those concepts into the courses, it may call out these true yearnings from the students, making their time in school or university the most satisfying to them. This could well be the true meaning in education.

Education is not about giving you the ability to make a $30,000 salary in the commercial sector or $50,000 salary in the financial sector. These are not the yardsticks. Universities should deliver "holistic education".

Aside from learning and development, students get to know a large group of peers as friends. Business school students will know their peers in business school. Language school students will know their fellow language school students. Teachers will invite guests from outside to come and speak to the students, and will link them up into such social networks. Gaining these important networks from both outside and within is not what students thought they would have as they started university education, although these definitely are their needs.

As you go and look for work, do you think you can get your desired jobs by just knowing some elementary knowledge in accounting, finance, and commercial laws, etc. that you have learned? Do you realize that employers may see soft skills as more important? Among others, they will assess your people skills, thinking process, ethical standards and attitude. Even some wish to know who you know, so your networks could be a great advantage there too.

Few students would mention those needs before they start university. The old needs of the old Left Circle are about career and work. Once they come in, they start to realize that studying is not only to satisfy the old needs. Now, their needs are expanded, including the soft skills and social networks we just mentioned. They may also have demands on practical issues concerning the environment, such as the dormitory, canteen and campus surroundings. These are new realizations in needs that we should take care of.

Are universities just here to satisfy students? What other roles can universities play for other groups or wider society? These new groups are the new Left Circles. Whenever society comes across certain issues, reporters often go to the universities and ask their professors for their views: "From a scholar's point of view, how do you see this matter?" Universities did not plan to take up this role, but these expectations have been gradually developed as the new Left Circle. They expect the academics to help by providing their unbiased and educated views.

As educators, we can easily be asked by a stranger to give advice: "Professor, what recommendations would you give my son who will go into university?" Should educators take up the role as consultant as well? Should we be the voice for the public on fairness and kindness? Should we be trend-leaders? These expectations from the wider society go beyond teaching and research duties written on our job descriptions. So, now you realize that a university is more than a university. Universities can have much broader functions. The scope can go further and further out, extending from near neighbourhoods to as far as the whole society.

Going a step further, should universities be concerned about the environment? We have to. If we as educators ignore the need of environmental protection, how can we be role models for the youngsters? How can we take up a leadership role? We were not given that duty when we started our job, but this is a new Left Circle for us. We believe we should take up all these new subject-matters because we know we have to go with the times, and more pertinently, to demonstrate our own Left-Right Circles theory in action.

Teachers have to first impart principles of good character. Otherwise, with business skills but immoral behaviours, students can cause a lot of harm to society. Moral education is a new need of the old Left Circle. For the teachers to use their position to give society good knowledge and a voice towards good social ethos, it is a new Left Circle being nurtured. For certain occasions, we may just be invited to speak about management theories, but we can extend it to giving speeches on life philosophies, hoping that we can touch and enlighten more people. In this way, we are in touch with a new Left Circle.

Going this way, we will find a lot of space to progress. But that does not mean we can now relax in our original duties. We cannot be found tardy and not giving our all in our teaching job. Our students will not respect us even when we are known for giving good speeches. If we fail to be good at our job, we will lose the crucial Left-Right Circles connecting point in creating and disseminating knowledge.

It is now very easy to differentiate between the three levels of Left Circle. Have you done your basic duty (old needs in old Left Circle)? Have you got additional duties to fulfil (new needs in old Left Circle)? Have you opened up new areas or even new segments (new Left Circles)? Following this thought process, you will find an open sky in front of you.

Some conservative people express their reservations about the usefulness of MBA and EMBA programmes. They believe that information is now easily accessible through the internet, and efforts for those courses are not justified. But what they forget is that the interactions between the teacher and students are the sources of inspiration and creativity. The sparks that are produced between the teacher and students are not limited to words but also include looks, smiles and gestures. All these can be translated into signals of praise, encouragement or push for more in the eyes of the students.

The teacher needs to use only a few words to start a whole in-depth discussion. We have this understanding from the Chinese proverb: "A book does not give all that needs to be said, and saying does not give all that needs to be understood." Those few words by the teacher are never enough to give the full meaning. One-way teaching using just books and words has very limited impact. Those are for the fundamental levels. Like emails being less effective than phone calls and phone calls being less effective than face-to-face meetings, we need good interactions to effectively convey meanings. To exploit the space in business education development, interactions are the most promising aspect to add value.

University teachers have to bear in mind what they are good at. Your unique skill is in the cross fertilization of knowledge and concept. This creates new angles and ideas. You should harness your strength to counter the weakness of the online network. If you give only written replies to your students, the time you write a reply may be the time they are sleeping. When they see your reply, their attention may have been drawn to other matters. It would be a pity if teachers do not use their advantage of interactivity with their students.

Interactivity can satisfy other needs. If a student wants to do a special research on a subject, he comes and talks to you, and then decides to change to another topic more suitable to him. This results in much better work from him. Your valuable input is not what a search engine can provide. If you cannot satisfy those needs, you are prone to be replaced by new technologies, and you will find it difficult to land a good job. When we work, we have to put our mind in for quality and new ideas. In accounting, for example, if you routinely process words and numbers without a method to ensure an understanding of the whole gist, you are bound to make a lot of mistakes.

Some teachers will resist such an approach. They think their duty is just to teach, and people should not expect them to spend time with students after class. Looking for jobs is a responsibility of the students', and they can go to the support office if they need help. If those teachers hold an attitude like this, I do not think they can even satisfy the old needs of the old Left Circle. While the students have expectations, the Right Circle is now too far from them. The teacher may be totally ignorant of what the job market demands these days, and his *modus operandi* is to deliver scripted lessons. He is completely detached from the real world. Teachers of that kind are resting on their laurels. University education to them is a formality. They are using a non-functioning format that is destined for decline.

How an industry ends up often depends on the mindset of the people. In his book *How the Mighty Fall,* author Jim Collins points out that when a stagnant industry is under assault by emerging ones, the situation is similar to someone being attacked by viruses. If he ignores it, he will get sicker and sicker until he is completely bedbound. Still, if he does not care, he will go on to the final stage beyond any treatment.

To avoid getting into those situations, firstly, you have to check if you are satisfying the old needs of your old Left Circle. Then, you will have to look after the new needs of your old Left Circle, including those needs your customers are unable to spell out to you clearly. Finally, you have to find your new Left Circles.

Case 6: Social Media

We now come to our final case — social media. The social media started with rather small coverage and functionality. It allowed people to tell where they have been and who they have met, etc., functioning very much like a photo album. But its spread and development has been astounding, capitalizing on the networks of friends (and of friends' friends) to quickly and widely disseminate information. Users can also do derivative work characterizing and retouching original photos, generating exponential propagation power. Then, what exactly is taking us to this situation? Is it the power of technology or our own needs that prompt us to use the technology? I think it is the mixture of both. If we are not receptive to the technology, no matter how powerful it is, the effort will not bear fruit.

The old need of the old Left Circle in social media is to read other people's status and distribute your own. But just to explore new needs of the old Left Circle, there is already a lot of room to work with. What are those new needs? Apart from wanting to know what others are doing, we wish also to see interactions of people in the form of comments. As part of our duty, we have produced materials that we hope to positively influence the general value system.

Influences can be good or bad. What we hope, of course, is to produce positive influence, such as encouraging people to learn and improve themselves. How do we encourage people to learn? We are sure we will get zero effect if we simply tell people "to learn and improve yourself" repeatedly. Instead, we believe we can talk about the different ways of learning. For instance, after listening to a speech, we can disseminate some content of the speech to let other people know in which areas they can work to lift themselves. People who are interested will come to us for more in the speech and perhaps ask who the speaker is. If permitted, we can also make referrals for direct contact.

We cannot just use "social" and "media" to explain what the social media does. It is a lot more complicated than that. It serves not only a socialization purpose using the electronic media, but it also embraces a sense of "being there". Why do people make posts on Facebook? Does it involve an intent of telling people that "I am here"? If you have not posted anything for the past few days, would people think that you have disappeared? This may have prompted you to post your whereabout. The matter also involves a desire to share, or an effort to maintain popularity. You just tell people how you have been irrespective of whether they are listening. But when you post a comment like "Sunset is ever so beautiful, only that night impends as dusk falls", the response you hope will be "hoping for a better tomorrow". The reaction can go either way — distressed or encouraged!

Going deeper into people's mentality associated with the social media, what are the needs of this generation on socialization? Do you want to know what people you do not know are doing? Do you want to make use of the speed and width of the network to distribute your information far and wide? But these ever-expanding needs and desires may bring unintended consequences that call for some conditioning through a code of conduct or social understanding, such as following some social etiquette. Where would the social media go looking ahead? Will it converge into another system? Will it trigger political movements? Will it inspire the pursuit of dream and perfection and deeper appreciation of life values? The sky is even wider for social media than for business education. And to be a bit wry, all we can say is: "The sky is the only limit."

The rapid development of social media has drawn in an increasing amount of needs. While many new needs emerge in the old Left Circle, new Left Circles also come on the scene in large numbers. As there is obviously much the sector can do, competition is also keen giving rise to a great variety of platforms. The most popular platforms today are Facebook, Weibo, Instagram and Twitter, etc. Platforms have to maintain their momentum to keep alive their old Left Circles while looking for ways to develop new Left Circles. This gives some food for thought for the people engaged in social media.

Summary

We start from satisfying old needs of the old Left Circle. We move on to explore new needs of the old Left Circle. Then, we go and develop new Left Circles. If you can discern clearly what these three levels involve, you will see a picture full of opportunities. It may be too simplistic to just talk about being "guided by the Left Circle". You need to ask yourself these questions: Are you getting your old Left Circle in good order? Are there opportunities for new needs you have not yet dealt with in the old Left Circle? Who are the ones that can be your new Left Circle? Only three questions are needed to lineate the general situation you are in.

You ask yourself again. Do you have new customers coming? Do you receive complaints from your old customers? Have you responded well to your customers' suggestions? Then, do your customers have new needs? You may not be aware that your customers can be satisfied by these other things. They may come to tell you what they want, or you can go and tell them your new ideas. All these exchanges give you food for thought, helping you with new theories and strategies. This is a good framework for you with which to decide on the right things to do.

If you get lost in the idea of the new Left Circle, you will come into a situation that is depicted in the book *Why the Mighty Fall*. You have to quickly rethink, remodel and revise your working model. As long as there are people out there, there will be needs for you to satisfy. Opportunities abound in all aspects of life, whether they be for life essentials, healthcare, education or entertainment.

Chapter 5

Internal Left Circle: Important Roles of Company's Own Staff

Left Circle inside the Company — More Complicated Than Customers

There exists a very important concept within the Left-Right Circle theory, called the "Internal Left Circle". What is the Internal Left Circle? The Left Circle concept is geared towards customers outside the company. Most of the time, we treat ourselves inside our own company as one unit. We then consider how as a unit we can satisfy the needs of the people outside. Taking this concept as the foundation, we now look at what we can do inside the company.

Consider yourself as the manager of a company. Who are the people in your company? You are one of them, of course, but there are also others in the same organization. You need to understand these people in terms of their needs, demands, personalities, behaviours, conditions and feelings. In this way, you work to make your staff happy, enabling the company to run smoothly. The company in turn gets all the skills and capabilities to make customers satisfied.

You may look at a staff and easily see if he is sick, but some conditions are difficult to notice, as many people are good at concealing their feelings without giving out any signs. The other problem may be that you even have problems understanding what you yourself need. People usually know what they do not like, but when asked what they like, many have difficulties giving a clear answer. This is much like the Left Circle outside — customers only see that the product rolled out is what they like, but not before.

But why do we put people in the company into one group, classify them as a separate category, and call them the "Internal Left Circle"? That is because the relationship between you and your staff is not a transactional one in nature. Against the Left Circle outside, however, the relationship can mostly be handled through our traditional marketing tools.

For example, if we are not interested in a certain market segment, we do not have to sell the product to them. We do not even have to set up sales channels for this segment. We do not have to present our product to this group because they are not our target. We can also set our prices to exclude them. Most importantly, the product design will differentiate the targets and non-targets. An example of this is that we do not use our university class format for primary school.

The way we deal with our Internal Left Circle is more complicated than for the External Left Circle against whom we can use our traditional marketing tools. For instance, there are people who were already in the company before you joined, and you cannot just get rid of them all. The handling is more difficult, because you have a lot more factors to consider.

Who will take over their jobs? How would your own boss see the whole matter? Who will look after the people whose bosses you have fired, and how would they see the whole issue? Who would look after their customers? Remember, your relationship with your Internal Left Circle is not transactional. It is more difficult than you can handle your External Left Circle. You cannot just say, "You are not my target, and I don't sell to you." You cannot do as you wish because there are a lot of other concerns.

Facing the External Left Circle, as long as you have a good product, the right price, comprehensive sales channels and effective promotional campaigns, you are very much on target and your customers are more or less looked after. But then you have a certain staff, and you know very little about what he exactly thinks. Can a certain salary level be sufficient as a way to satisfy him? You may think that money is all-powerful: "With money, you can be as wilful as you want." Unfortunately, you will find that "price" is in fact a weak factor to influence you staff.

It does not mean that you need not pay your staff salaries — you must — but money is not all that will make your staff stay and work. Would money alone be able to motivate your staff to give their all to the company? Can you treat your staff any way you want after you pay them salaries? Can high pay and fat bonus be good enough when people do not see prospects of improvement and advancement? If your business is unethical, would people of high moral principle want to work for you?

The Internal Left Circle and External Left Circle are similar yet different. The Internal Left Circle and the company are all but one unit, so your considerations become a lot more complicated. You do not have as much space to use compared with outside. It is easier with your customers because you can choose, but for the Internal Left Circle, you are not as free.

Example 1: Your boss's secretary. Can you choose who? Do you want to work with her? Can you affect the salary she receives? Can you fire her? It is not easy even to establish a good working relationship with her. To the External Left Circle, you can place them higher on your target list or use a new selling point to attract them, and they will likely stay with you. But to someone like your boss's secretary, she may remember you have uttered some words that she did not like five years ago, and you have great difficulties to change that perception.

Example 2: Your staff. People have their own strengths and weaknesses. A certain sales staff has been very considerate towards customers and promised them something that the company has difficulties in fulfilling. The other colleagues are not happy with his decision and believe that he has not got the balance right. Even with such a mistake, can you just fire him? When you get rid of him, you get rid of his strengths too.

Example 3: New recruits. When you hire, can you ascertain who is promising and who is not? In a half-hour interview, can you go deep into knowing the candidate's personality and attitude? The best you can do is to use a prescribed list to assess his general skills and strong points. What is even more difficult is to look at a person's potentials. When queried why he has not done anything to prove himself, he may say that it is exactly why he wants a job giving him the opportunities to show what he can. How do you make a judgement on that? If you only hire people with proven records, you may be too conservative and are prone to missing out on yet-to-realize potentials and new ideas that your company needs.

To get along well with the Internal Left Circle is not an easy thing, and there are no fixed rules. Just as in Example 2 above, a colleague may be too eager to please the customers and promise things that are beyond the company's ability. But the other side of the equation could be that your company is too rigid in its policies, and if the colleague is equally rigid, we will never be able to cut a deal.

We can see the dilemma here. If we ask for a change in the company's policies, we may be going too far to upset too many people. We may not get approvals from above. Or, we do not have the required quality from our existing employees to execute the change. Or, our IT systems are not able to handle the requirements. Those are real and very valid reasons, but if we care too much about our Internal Left Circle, we may continue to miss out on opportunities from the External Left Circle, thereby weakening our competitiveness.

Managers and staff may constantly face this problem. Bosses want to move forward as fast as we can, but staff may see such demands as "not what they have signed up for". Who is right and who is wrong? There are no hard and fast answers. It requires a balance to be found somewhere. As we said, all these Internal Left Circle issues come as more complicated than facing the External Left Circle.

When you manage your Internal Left Circle well, bringing about an amicable atmosphere and making everybody go in the same direction, this becomes your very strong Right Circle. This is the power you have to attract External Left Circles. Conversely, if conflicts and disputes happen all the time within, then your Right Circle is all but non-functioning. When we think everything is ready, you find you are without your flyers and advertisement boards for the marketing campaign, and you will be upset. You find out that it is because someone in your Internal Left Circle who is not happy with you has not followed up with the production company. That is not a strong Right Circle. Without a strong Right Circle, you cannot make your External Left Circle happy.

"Internal" includes not only employees. When you are bothered with all things that happen at work, you may get another blow from another important part of your Internal Left Circle — your family. You better half may ask, "Why do you work that hard? Can you come back earlier for the children? Can you spend more time with me? We have not had a trip for a long time." Now, you are caught between a rock and a hard place. Now, you also know why we need to discuss Internal Left Circle.

We should have enough materials for a Left-Right Circles book just about family. You can fire your employees, but you cannot do the same with your children. You do not want to separate with your spouse. You do not renounce your relationship with your parents. How would you handle a dispute between you better half and your parent? Your parents, your spouse and your children are all in your Internal Left Circle. How do you balance out the whole situation with conflicts of interest? How do you avoid mishaps that upset harmony, just as simple as making a choice of restaurant? You need to consider your position very carefully among the many interests and demands.

The age-old question for the husband is: "Who do you rescue first, your wife or your mother?" People are faced with dilemmas all the time. The best strategy perhaps is to take steps to avoid it from the very beginning. For the husband in the above case, perhaps it is best for him to take the relationship to a satisfactory level that questions like the one above will not be asked at all. Instead, you get appreciation of how good you have been as a husband. You do not want to get to the situation where this question needs to be asked.

We will do a brief summary here. For a company, we have many Left Circles outside. We need to organize and move our Right Circle to satisfy their needs. Moving the Right Circle involves a lot of people, including your colleagues, your bosses and the bosses of your bosses, etc. There are also people influencing your bosses that you need to take into consideration as well — all of these to be covered in the next Chapter "Left Circle of Left Circle". The ways you are going to deal with these people are going to be very different.

Firstly, you cannot define who is of the highest priority for you in your Internal Left Circle. You cannot put these people in an order of importance per se. Whether it is your peers, your bosses or your subordinates, they can be equally crucial to you.

Secondly, against your Internal Left Circle, you have to take a long-term view. Customers come and buy things from you, and it can be a short-term or a long-term relationship. But for your Internal Left Circle, you will run into trouble if you make mistakes in treating them. For a lasting relationship, you need a complete view of all aspects that bring you the desired result.

Thirdly, your choices and spheres of influence against your Internal Left Circle are very different from your External Left Circle. For a lot of those who exist in your Internal Left Circle, you do not have a choice about whether they should be there. For them, what you can influence (including their promotions and salary adjustments) is at best indirect, meaning that you have no direct influence.

How To Ascertain Mindsets and Needs of Internal Left Circle

It raises a question: How can we ascertain the needs of the Internal Left Circle?

The first step is actually to ask yourself: Are you interested in understanding the needs of the Internal Left Circle? Do you accept this is your responsibility? Do you recognize that if your Internal Left Circle is mishandled, this will affect the External Left Circle? You have to believe that the Internal Left Circle is very important and you need to take up the responsibility of understanding if the people around you are happy. If you see any signs of people being unhappy and you choose to ignore them, you will definitely run into serious problems. When people start making their dismay explicit through words and actions, chances are it will be very difficult now to deal with their grievances and return the situation back to normal. Just as if you ignore your early signs of sickness, you can be sure you will get very sick.

If you have no idea if your people are satisfied, you are unable to move your Right Circle. In fact, you may just have no intention to move your Right Circle. To get an understanding of your Internal Left Circle, there are a few ways. The first is the most direct in that observations can be applied to see if the person is customarily late, spends not enough time at work and deliberately delays or slows things down. Some people may pretend that he is working very hard, but he is simply procrastinating. Some people just spend their time at work without giving out their all. All these behaviours can be gauged through observations.

You can use your ears to hear as well. You ask a staff member, "How's everything today?" He replies, "It's just work. What do you expect?" This sort of negative tone shows his state of mind. This reply can be a bit more cordial: "It's a bit chilly outside. Make sure you have enough on, Professor!" It reflects a more uplifting mood. Then, you ask, "How are the students?" His reply could be: "Every student is a bit naughty. We were naughty too when we were young." Now, you have to discern if this is courtesy or it contains other meanings. If he follows it by: "I don't know how to deal with these kids!", then you know you need to get up and take action. For someone to bring out a problem even in such a subtle form, you have to take it as a problem you have to solve now for the organization.

Apart from your eyes and ears, you have sensing abilities. As you get close to a person, you can sense his magnetism aura. Only if you close your own sensing abilities will you not get the messages. By shutting off, you simply do not care what is happening to other people. Magnetism sensing is not anything mysterious. It is about the messages sent through a person's temperament. Some appear to be very kind and caring, while others look very domineering and intimidating. As people are also affected by recent happenings and his own health conditions etc., he can display different auras under different conditions.

The reactions that are visible are easier to detect. What is difficult to know is his inner world. We have to approach it from theories. Many theories touch upon people's motivation. The common one that has been mentioned is Maslow's Hierarchy of Needs. Readers can go through some of these theories and apply them for Internal Left Circle issues.

We go to the first and basic level of Maslow's Hierarchy of Needs: physiological needs. For companies to satisfy employees' first level of needs, salaries or wages have to be paid. Not paying wages of course would result in very angry employees ending up with the employees leaving. To pay a wage level below subsistence will also cause employees to leave.

The second level is security needs. This concerns how certain employees will receive their wages. Some bosses may tell their employees that they cannot guarantee on-time payment because the company is in financial difficulties. When they say so, what do their employees think? The bosses might take it for granted that employees will see this as reasonable and accept to help the company out. But the message is that the company is in dire straits, which is extremely damaging. It also means that the company is badly run. Employees will think that they may have to go down with the company. In this situation, it is difficult to expect the employees to have any patience to wait the company to reset its Left-Right Circles.

The third level of social or belonging needs is very crucial. If a person in a company believes that he does not belong there and only operates as his individual self, he will not be happy. His feeling could be that the company does not value him as a person and is only buying his time. Work nature or content can also affect the sense of belonging too. If I work 20–30 years in the same company on the same type of job, I can hardly see this as a development. My interest can hardly be maintained. If the boss disregards the development of a sense of belonging, the whole group will suffer.

Satisfying Maslow's first three levels of needs is already difficult, but if your company can advance to fulfilling the top two levels, it will prove your company an excellent one. It means your employees feel they have self-dignity and self-fulfilment. The best scenario is that not just a few but most of your employees feel that they have those higher needs satisfied. Many nations impart a sense of glory to their soldiers through their military training programmes, making them feel they have a sense of duty to protect the country. This pushes their morale up and induces courage in them to the extent of dying for the country. This is a good application of fulfilling Maslow's two highest levels of needs.

Generally, businesses do not have to take the military management model. The key is to make everybody feel the warmth within. It always takes time to reach higher levels, as Rome was not built in one day. You need patience to face your Internal Left Circle. As your experience and high intelligence give you the ability to take up a management position, you can lead by these very qualities rather than subject staff to the harsh measures such as censure, punishment and control. If you treat your staff harshly, they will feel extremely insecure.

If you manage to cultivate an amicable and amiable environment at your workplace, your colleagues will never shy away from work. They will see the workplace as a happy place comparable to playing with their children. How can we nurture such a workplace and very committed colleagues? We can certainly take a leaf from Maslow to effectively apply his theories.

Discerning Negative Signs in Internal Left Circle

Understanding how crucial the Internal Left Circle is to the company, are there ways to restore performance when signs of deterioration are seen? Once you see a drop in performance, you will have to trace the source and understand what causes the drop. Is it that your staff is given a job that is beyond his ability or is it that his own resistance has caused him to give up putting in his best? A self-talk like this does not help with the motivation: "I can certainly do it, but I just don't want to. What can you do to me?"

After an assessment on the employee's side, the next is to do the same on the company's side. Could the existing system be causing low spirits among employees? Could it be that while individuals are putting in hard work, it is the entire work environment that is causing the poor performance? Perhaps, the culprit is the excessive interference from above or the poor coordination between departments. Do we provide requisite rewards for good-performing staff? Are those rewards fair? If as a boss you tell them, "Just do it for the group. Everybody is doing the same." It can be true, but can also be too true as to discourage the staff concerned by ignoring or playing down their extra contributions.

Then, it is also the question of whether the rewards given are what the receiver sees as important. Pay is important, but people are also looking for growth and development. Even further, they may hope for making a contribution to the wider society. Rewards can be classified into intrinsic and extrinsic types. Extrinsic rewards are visible and concrete, such as a letter of appreciation from you, the boss. But can work itself provide meanings to the staff concerned? If there is any self-satisfaction generated from work, it is an intrinsic reward.

Intrinsic rewards weigh higher than extrinsic rewards from the staff's point of view. Self-motivation is higher as driven by intrinsic rewards. If someone wants to try something new, hoping that it will help push the boundaries, a few words like these will surely set him back: "Don't be silly! The boss will not approve it." The whole enthusiasm will be pushed back. If this happens frequently, he will not be motivated to continue offering anything productive. Why should he remain here? Even if there are extrinsic rewards they receive from salaries and words of appreciation, still you cannot expect their performance to be driven too much higher.

Apart from poor performance, the other negative reaction is resignation. When a colleague wants to go for another job, this gives the company a warning. It tells the company to reflect: where are we short to cause this resignation? To address the Internal Left Circle problems, it counts on us to regularly self-reflect on how we have been treating our colleagues and subordinates. You have to remember: the Left Circle consistently moves left, and the Internal Left Circle is no different. When you find a certain staff is happy this year, it does not mean he will be equally happy next year. You can give him all the extrinsic rewards that you can muster, but the lack of intrinsic reward will still prompt him to go eventually.

Given the high positions intrinsic rewards hold in employees, companies should engage staff more using values and allow for better fits with staff's own purposes. This is clever management. If staff see that they will not have the same chance elsewhere of doing the things they value, they will stay put and not be enticed by a higher pay elsewhere. If they mind too much about pay levels, then it shows that there are already problems in management.

When the company uses their values to achieve coherence, how should it handle those employees whose values are not in sync with the company's? For the unsalvageable, the company should let them go naturally, in an orderly way and without any fuss. For those who are deemed changeable, the company should arrange to help them to make the necessary adjustment such that they will be back as useful assets for the company.

Even for those who look to have no problem, the company cannot just sit on its laurels. Little chips light great fires. Management should act on any signs of discontent on the staff's part. Management should clearly explain the company's directions to the employees and show that they also understand the employees' difficulties with a firm commitment to resolve issues together. The Internal Left Circle presents considerable challenges to management owing to its complexity and intricacy, and the matter cannot be taken lightly.

Problems at the Internal Left Circle warrant more of our thought than for the External Left Circle. Why? A staff switching to another company faces more difficulties and possibly a higher personal cost than a customer moving to another service provider. You have to do a deeper reflection on why an employee still wants to leave facing such difficulties.

Potentially, someone departing the Internal Left Circle will have a significant effect on the rest of the Internal Left Circle, particularly when the staff concerned is regarded as a good employee. It would be better if, say, it is a retirement. Yet, even that, you still have to do a review. If you do not know why someone is leaving, then you are in a trouble spot because the person would not leave for no reason, only that he is not telling you. The other reason why you need to review is that one person at the Internal Left Circle handles a number of External Left Circles, and a person who departs your Internal Left Circle affects you more than a customer who departs your External Left Circle.

To develop an ability in self-reflection, you can study theories, or accumulate experiences, or get help from your network. Do you have people around you who can give you good advices? Do you accept what they advise you? If you take an attitude in "I need no one to tell me what to do because I am a lot more qualified than anyone", then it is not just dangerous but extremely damaging to your Internal Left Circle. The more arrogant you are, the more difficult you will find it in understanding your Internal Left Circle. You shut people out in your problem-solving process, which will only bring you disastrous outcomes before you realize it.

Here we only talk about your Internal Left Circle in the work environment. We have not touched upon family, public service or church. Situations there are even more complex. At work, you have wages that help you hold on to your staff, but these other settings have no wages involved. If you cannot handle your work environment well even with the help of wages, then you know how difficult it is to handle your family without any stick or carrot. There is no way you can threaten your children by taking away their lifeline.

Maintaining Harmony in Internal Left Circle

It is seldom that you find an organization is operated by one person. What if people in an organization do not embrace each other and instead indulge in conflicts all the time? Education needs to go all around within an organization — between superiors, colleagues and subordinates. Each person needs to learn how to be tolerant. Money cannot do the trick. People need to realize that they are all on the same boat, and working together is the best way to attain their mutual purpose.

Birds of a feather flock together. The people who get around you are mostly those with similar views and ideas. So, instead of getting people all of the same type to work in an organization, you need a common denominator to bind all different people together. You need to find and set a purpose for the organization that everybody knows and agrees to. If your purpose is to maximize profits by any means, then probably all the ethical people in your Internal Left Circle will leave. They will not find your purpose congruent with theirs. When there are no clear standards specified above, you will not get the quality you want below. A lot of organizations fail because people are unclear about the real purpose and meaning, and they are unable to turn their energy towards one clear direction.

At what time should you explain the company's mission to your employees? Any time, in fact. But to different levels of staff, you need different methods. For the basic level staff, they will not get what you want if you start with your great philosophy. You would probably say, "Thank you for being part of us. You will have some duties to perform, and this is how we divide the work. Your part is very important, and we trust you are more than capable to fulfil these duties. The company will see your development as very important, because it is only when you grow can we grow too." The key here is that it has to be a language that your staff can understand. Some do not need further explanation, while others may just do what they are asked to because they see your sincerity.

At times, you see some people not getting up to speed, and you may be upset. But remember, getting upset will not help you, your staff, your department or your company. All you need is just to carry on with your sincerity and benevolent approach and continue developing your staff. In managing your reaction, you are training yourself to be of good temperament. If you can put away your anger and focus on the people or issue at hand, you are cultivating a character in you that will go to another level. You will find yourself much better at handling the Left-Right Circles issues.

Interpersonal relationship is a difficult matter. Jealousy is all around. Good-performing staff may be envied. Yet, poor-performing staff may also get despised. Grudges may surface between colleagues owing to their differences in views and methods. There can be a lot of personality clashes happening. All these are very difficult matters to sort out.

As bosses, we may not be able to understand all factors behind the conflicts. Some bosses choose to pretend nothing has ever happened, thinking that those involved will find their ways around the matter. In fact, they were afraid to get involved and get caught in the middle. Some other bosses would choose to just do patch-up work without going into the crux of the issue, asking staff to put the matter behind quickly and focus on work. Yet, are these the solutions to the problems?

How can we unite people together in a company? Relationships within our Internal Left Circle are changing all the time. Two people can be arguing fiercely in the day, while they just go and play football after work as teammates. Colleagues can team up asking for raises and better benefits, but when they deal with the appropriation, they suddenly stand as enemies. People can be very unpredictable and can turn their backs on each other just over some trivial matters. These are things that give us great uncertainties in how we can get people to work together.

To maintain a cohesive Internal Left Circle, money is never enough. People do not flock to you because you have money. The issue involves a few complex elements. Firstly, every case is different, and you need to analyze the situation every single time. Secondly, the issue cannot be dealt with by money or traditional marketing tools. Thirdly, there is an element of education in your effort. You can indoctrinate your Internal Left Circle. Fourthly, the whole situation can change very rapidly.

A certain activity may be just what you need to turnaround something. Unlike the external Left Circle, you have a lot of opportunities within your Internal Left Circle for people to come together. Originally having a discord, two people may go to a birthday party and end up treating each other amicably. Occasions like visiting a sick friend or going to a funeral may suddenly bring a very different chemistry. You have those moments in your Internal Left Circle that you can use. The key is in how you exercise your disposition, knowledge, intelligence and kind-heartedness to create a positive effect.

You cannot totally control your Internal Left Circle. The corporate culture, who's who in the organization, education background and social norms all have influence on how people in Internal Left Circle think. In this smartphone era, there are demands that work does not have to be done in the office as long as the work is ultimately done. You have to make reference to those influences.

Do not despair when you find yourself making mistakes in managing your Internal Left Circle. The whole matter is very complex. The significance is not in how clever you are. If we put another person in your place, he may be making more mistakes. Should he be doing a better job than you, what you have to do is to go and learn from him. There is also an issue of long-term perspective versus short-term perspective. Something seems to have been settled, but there may remain a deep-seated root cause yet to be dealt with. If you take the short-term approach of going along with everything, you may see your cost up reaching unmanageable levels. Be aware that a temporary relief may bring serious long-term consequences.

No Golden Rule for Managing Internal Left Circle

In managing our Internal Left Circle, do we need a consistent set of standards over the handling of all people and matters? While systems and rules have their place in management, they are at best guidelines and points of reference. We need a more flexible approach to make judgement according to the situations at hand. This flexibility has to be exercised within reasons and within the principle of fairness, with a view to ensuring everyone is happy with the result. It is the spirit behind those rules and regulations that is the basis for exercising such flexibility.

Handling difficult situations requires some wisdom. For example, when a colleague of yours creates a big scene at the office, even damaging properties, would you simply dismiss him or report him to the police for his mistake? But before you do anything, you have to understand what happened to him. You understand from his last 20 years in the company that he does not have this behaviour, and it must have been some difficult situations he has been struggling with that triggered his outburst. He has to be a good employee because he came back for the urgent matter even when he is so unsettled. A gentle pat on his shoulder, plus some reassuring words should handle the matter. You simply assure him, "Anything we can help you with, my friend? I know how difficult it is to come back under these circumstances. Go back when you have this done!".

How do you balance between exercising flexibility and following the rules? When you set the rules, you should at the same time consider what flexibility you can exercise. And when you exercise flexibility, you also consider how it will not upset the validity of the rules. There are certainly exceptions to rules, but if you recklessly allow exceptions to be applied just as you wish, then you are defeating all the purposes of setting up the rules. People will have no guides to look to.

Rules and regulations have their functions, but they should also leave some leeway. Say, your dress code in the office is suit and tie. But if you are going down to the industrial area, would you still insist on the same dress code? You look a total misfit if you appear as such amidst a factory environment. To adjust between an office and a factory environment needs flexibility to be incorporated in the rules. So, on what basis should the balance be set between following the rules and exercising flexibility? It refers to the purpose of your company. As your company aims to satisfy needs of various Left Circles including your Internal Left Circle, different approaches are called for towards different groups. The level of flexibility needed lies in there.

Internal Left Circle for a Country or a Territory

All that is said here about the Internal Left Circle is not just a way for company management to appease their staff. It is indeed about achieving an environment of mutual appeasement that brings about a united front taking on a certain mission. Some say, "You cannot have two alphas in one group", so what you need are very delicate skills to ensure that persons with domineering character tone down their domination tendency and cooperate. The best method to lead people to accept cooperation is a powerful and inspiring vision. In the context of a country, this powerful and inspiring vision is to build a strong and prosperous country for all people.

You also need a variety of skills to form a good team. Do not look down upon some lesser skills — they may be the ones you need at some important juncture. If you do not tolerate certain idiosyncratic behaviours, you may be missing out on some important qualities or viewpoints that can be very useful. Accepting different strengths reflects a leader's broadmindedness. To get the respect of your people, you have to be fair and just, show that you act with both integrity and good ability, and explain clearly every important decision that you make.

To take the whole theory into the context of government administration, the external Left Circle for the government is all citizens and residents, and its Internal Left Circle is all the officials, government employees and political parties. For promoting the territory's interests to outside, the world becomes the External Left Circle and all citizens and residents are the Internal Left Circle. The government needs its Internal Left Circle to work closely together in order to make things happen.

On the political front, to get a unanimous view from everyone is not easy if not impossible, as political parties and different people all have their own concepts and ideologies. Looking forward, what should be the direction of the development in Hong Kong, in China and for the whole world? The blueprints are all different. There are always different voices in society, with a portion of the population not falling into the official line. A set of good values, a sense of mission and a powerful vision are very important tools that help bring the community together. Education plays an important role in instilling those values.

Things are never easy and may not happen just as we wish. Even so, we still need to be positive. We cannot give up. Even if all things go against you, you cannot simply say, "I'll join it if I cannot beat it." You have to stand your ground in remaining righteous and kind even if you are alone doing so. But things are never quite as hopeless as you think. You always have someone with you from your Internal Left Circle. They share your ideals and values. They can fight with you together. They are your strong Right Circle. There is righteousness in this world. The light will never go out. Take this mentality, and you will carry your mission on.

Chapter 6

Left Circle of Left Circle: Exploring and Capitalizing on People Influencing Left Circle

We explained the importance of the Left Circle in our previous chapters and pointed out that we can choose our Left Circles under certain circumstances. But our Left Circles also have their own Left Circles, and if we ignore those outer Left Circles, we would have problems satisfying the whole needs of the Left Circle. Each person should have more than one Left Circle throughout his life, and each of his Left Circles should also have multiple Left Circles. Facing that many Left Circles along with so many needs, we have to carefully find our own positioning and establish excellent relationships with our Left Circles.

Who Influence Your Left Circle?

Let us first explain what "Left Circle of Left Circle" is. This is an important part of the Left Circle theory. How is it important? The principles discussed in Chapters 1–4 are taken from marketing concepts at 1.0 and 2.0 levels. Marketing 1.0 is to produce products to attract customers to buy, which is sales-oriented. Meanwhile, Marketing 2.0 is to look at whether customers are satisfied and whether the products are useful to them, which is customer-oriented. These are traditional marketing methods that direct the Right Circle to move towards the Left Circle to satisfy its needs.

Your marketing acumen is not up-to-speed if you cannot elevate yourself to Marketing 3.0. At that level, your sight is not confined to the customers at hand but expanded to the whole ecosystem including the industrial chain and the entire community. To single-mindedly go for pampering your customers, your action may be a bit too far that may jeopardize the interests of your company or your suppliers. That is not Marketing 3.0. Even if the industrial chain is satisfied but the product causes social resentment or discontent in some segments, it is still not what it ought to be. Even when there is no immediate discontent but the product is found to have left adverse long-term consequence, it is still unsatisfactory.

"Marketing 3.0" is a very broad subject worthy of a separate book. As we delve into the Left Circle here, what we should know now is that it is not enough to just focus on the Left Circle itself. To embrace the whole Left Circle, we have to also understand the ecosystem that works behind. "Left Circle of Left Circle" is therefore an important area of this whole understanding.

From fancying something to eventually buying it, apart from the promotional message by the advertiser, the customer is influenced by a lot of other factors. If you do not consider those factors, only seeing that your price is what the customer cares, you have missed out a lot. If you think your product and your price are the only determining factors, you are at best only getting a part of the equation right. Think of yourself, do you simply buy because the product is good? We suggest no. Your decision is influenced by a lot of forces working around you.

Putting all the forces in an order of importance, normally you will find it is "people" that takes up the pole position. When you say it is a matter or a thing that affects you most, think about who makes that matter happen in the first place. Who puts that thing there? What forces are there that interact to form that situation? Many a time, it is people who are the real forces behind.

Since we are sure it is people that affect other people, we need to find out who is influencing our target customers in the Left Circle? Getting to this point, now we are entering the real essence of marketing — transcending Marketing 1.0 and Marketing 2.0 into Marketing 3.0. If you cannot get your understanding up to this intricate level that concerns an ecosystem and multiple lines of influence behind the purchase decision, your effort will end up a lot less effective. You can only rely on your Right Circle to try to create some limited effect.

A lot of thinking used for marketing development today is too straight-line. The concept cannot be based on one-to-one but one-to-many relationships. What you face is a strong Left Circle A. Behind this Left Circle A are a number of Left Circles AA, AB, AC, AD, etc., and behind AA are many more Left Circles AA1, AA2, etc.

In our Left-Right Circles theory, our job is to develop a complete understanding of the influences that affect a person's decision, whether the nature of that influence is conscious or subconscious. What a person does is affected by the people around him far more than just by the Right Circle. How much can your Right Circle do to influence the decision? Against your perception, it is actually not a lot. In this age of social media, there is little you can control over the information that is circulated and the public opinion that is formed. You may see public opinion as part of a distant general environment surrounding your business, but a lot of it actually comes from the people around your Left Circle. These people are your "Left Circle of Left Circle", or in short, "Left-Left".

The Left Circles of Car Buyers

For a business, Left-Left can be a source for life and death. Let us look at a few examples below.

A man intends to buy a car. He looks at the car's performance, price and style. He might even have a checklist to fact-check his wishes to determine his choice. But who will influence him in his car decision? Is it all paid for by himself or shared among the family? If money comes from the joint account with his wife, how much of her opinion comes into this decision? When she is part of the decision, does she think the same as her husband? Very likely not. She may look at the colour a lot more than the car's performance, fuel efficiency or easy handling. The first thing she looks at maybe is the number of seats that she considers for their children. The horsepower required to climb up the hill is secondary. The car dealer may not have met his wife, but he cannot ignore her presence in the context of this decision. Even if the husband alone can pay with his cheque book, his wife is still the Left-Left.

But the wife may not be the only Left-Left. Can his boss's car also influence his decision? As all his bosses are driving the same type of car, what will he choose? He may opt to buy two cars — one for work and one for the weekend — to satisfy his desire. And if his boss is driving a hybrid, symbolizing his environmental concern, it would seem naïve for him to choose a high fuel-consumption car. He may like a certain car himself, but he would possibly give it up because of other people. If he is buying the car for work, of course it will not be too much of his free choice.

Even when the Left-Left is not involved in the process — he does not contribute a cent to the purchase and may not have given a single comment, still it is an influence. If the buyer indeed asks his boss for his opinion and the boss assures him it is all his decision, we can still be quite sure he will not choose anything that outshines his boss. For the car dealer, he will not see his boss nor know everything that happens behind, but the influence is there. This whole concept of the influence that works behind a decision is called Left Circle of Left Circle.

You may have noticed that a lot of advertising is not targeting the users but some other people. People ask a car manufacturer why they advertise widely a beautiful and elegant car not really made for the general public. The manufacturer replies, "These advertisements feature how our car is meticulously made to elevate our image to the public as a prestigious carmaker."

Some people use their cars as a symbol of their status and wish to show how superior they are. "I am better because my car is bigger and longer. I am better because I have a newer car." When they have nothing else to show off, they use their cars. The other consumers are what they measure against. The other people become the Left Circle of Left Circle.

You are unable to solve a great deal of problems if you do not recognize the presence of Left-Left. People around you influence what you do and how you behave. If people speak badly about you, you land yourself in great troubles. When poor publicity starts to circulate around your product, even customers who used to like it will now reconsider if they are making a wise choice.

Someone is thinking seriously and passionately about getting a smart two-door sports car. But because of all the factors around him, he does not have a chance. Whenever he makes his desire known, he would be asked, "Do you intend to exclude your in-laws?" The in-laws would never be able to climb into the back seats of the small car. He also has kids, and he will be seriously warned: "Getting the kids to the back will be a nightmare every time!" He then suggests buying another car. "Do you have space for two cars?" Those messages never get to the car dealer, but this is what happens. If you do not consider the Left-Left in your marketing, you will never come to the leading edge.

In our world of business, there are some unrealistic thoughts. Some marketers think that an outstanding product is what it takes to capture the market, or the product would automatically sell when they have established themselves with superb positioning, marketing campaigns and sales channels. This is obviously not the case. They have to see it from the ecosystem point of view and understand the conditions under which people are using the car. A lot of sales efforts become futile because the pitches do not point rightly at the conditions under which the car is used.

What the salesperson was told is probably that the car is used mostly for going to the golf course. But in fact, what is not known is a family of four will be carried to the golf course. So, the assumption that it only needs space for the golf clubs is wrong. When it is used to transport the whole family, there will also be four different perceptions that need to be managed. Even a fifth may exist when occasionally his friend comes with him in the car. When he buys the car, it is bought with the interests of other users in mind too. All these other users are the Left-Left. They would not appear before you, but if you do not know their influences, you will find it difficult to get the deal done.

Who Are Intel's Targets in the Left Circle?

The car example above belongs to a category known as B2C (business-to-consumer). Let us go to an example that is B2B (business-to-business). Intel Corporation is the world leading producer of central processing units (CPUs) for personal computers. It is famous for its trademark slogan "Intel Inside®" as well. Every computer using the Intel chip has a sticker with this trademark on it. What does Intel Inside® mean for the consumers? Most people have very little knowledge about chips, but they have a great positive image of the product. When they do not see the sticker on the computer, their immediate response is: "this computer does not have Intel Inside®".

Intel Inside® is a message that has made it into people's hearts and minds. But are the consumers Intel's Left Circle? Intel does not sell chips directly to consumers. It sells to the computer manufacturers who in turn assemble computers and sells the machines to the public. To Intel, the computer manufacturers are its Left Circle. The consumers are therefore Intel's Left-Left. So, when Intel designs its campaigns and puts in resources to promote Intel Inside®, who is it targeting — the computer manufacturers or the consumers? This is the key point.

When people decide that they have to buy a computer with Intel Inside®, even the manufacturers who are the computer experts cannot stop them. Given the tremendous efforts required, the manufacturers do not see it a need to change people's mind. They can go along. After all, Intel's chips are superior in quality supported by good marketing and excellent reputation and image. When the Left-Left is happy with Intel, the Left Circle would not have much problem using its product. Having said all this, we wish to make a note that we are not promoting Intel here, just using it as an example to illustrate our theory.

Why do other companies not do as Intel does? Intel's action comes from its very special status. Only when Intel has such a dominating position in the market can it use this strategy to target the general consumers. To do so, it takes a lot of money to run campaigns. You have to be very strong and powerful to be able to come to this effect. It is said that when Intel first thought of doing this, it had clashed with IBM on the issue. Eventually, it succeeded in putting its Intel Inside® sticker on the computers. Without its extraordinary strength, it would not have established itself so well.

When you are not as powerful as Intel, you have to first determine which Left Circle you want to serve. You pinpoint a specific market as well. For example, if we choose to run a private kitchen, we are targeting specific customers who want something more than the food you find everywhere. But we still choose this market even when we know we are serving only one family a night. For that, we do not have to run big campaigns, and we can simply count on referrals, or word-of-mouth, to get business. The people who recommend our service to other people are our Left-Left.

If you are just using a simple theory of Left Circle to run your business, you are limited. As you raise your level in the Left Circle theory, you find you are not only facing one but multiple Left Circles. You have to satisfy many customers at the same time, including those you have no chance of seeing but they exist. Those customers are your Left-Left. As you know they exist, you have to find ways to satisfy them so as to get their influence that you want on the customers that you can see and are in contact with. This is the intricacy resident in the "Left Circle of Left Circle" theory.

Internal Left Circle is Equally Influenced by Others

Next, we are going to talk about how to utilize the Left Circle of Left Circle concept in the work environment as we face our Internal Left Circle. Assuming you are a mid-level manager in a company, and you want a link with the CEO because you want to impress him and establish yourself in the company with your brilliant proposal. What does the CEO want? How good is your Right Circle that can meet the needs of this Internal Left Circle? At this stage, you are along the line of Marketing 2.0.

However, you also have to ponder who would influence the CEO. As you do not report directly to the CEO, the chance of going directly to him is slim, with 3–4 levels of reporting in-between. Even if you think you have a great recommendation to make, you still have to go through the layers, especially your immediate superior, the Marketing Director. You do want your great idea to be taken up by the CEO, because you do see your proposition as one of a kind and it should not be lost in the layers ending up in the waste bin. As you have confidence that the CEO will see your proposal positively, what you want is to at least have your proposal come in front of him without being blocked by the people in-between. These people may not be against you, but there exist many factors such as their considerations of risk, etc.

In a situation as complex as this, who is your Left Circle? Can you not regard your immediate superior as your Left Circle? You certainly cannot leave him out because you will not be able to have your proposal sent to the CEO if you do not get his endorsement. But of course, the CEO is definitely your Left Circle because your ultimate wish is to have your proposal accepted by him. As the CEO makes the final decision, your direct Left Circle is the CEO. However, your immediate superior is also your Left Circle because he does have the power to stop everything from happening.

So, who indeed is your Left Circle, and who is your Left-Left? A method like this will help you make the judgement: Which Left Circle is the closest to your desired final destination? The one who finally approves and makes your dream come true is your Left Circle. Under this logic, the CEO is your Left Circle, his decision being the finality you are looking forward to. While the position your immediate superior takes can have a big influence on the final outcome, he is not the final decision-maker per se. You do need his help in the process in the form of an endorsement or recommendation, or at least a no-objection, so he is your Left-Left.

Apart from your immediate superior, are there any more Left-Lefts you have to consider? While the responsibility to approve your proposal rests with the CEO, most likely he will need endorsement from the Chairman as well. But the CEO is still your Left Circle because he holds the key role in pushing your proposal through the whole organization. The Chairman has a view on the proposal which the CEO respects, so he is also the Left-Left that you have to address. While you would address your proposal to the CEO, you may want to include certain statements aimed at the Chairman. You have thought about the concerns of the Chairman, and put in some precautionary measures such as a full financial forecast to address his concerns.

We have described two Left-Lefts — your immediate superior and the Chairman. The situation is even more complicated when you notice there are other seemingly insignificant people who can have influence too. These people do not have the official power but they can have influence one way or another. They can be your good Left-Lefts. These people can be the driver, the secretary, opinion leaders and seniors in the company. While the seniors may not hold a formal position, the Chairman may still consult them. You cannot ignore these Left-Lefts. For example, your proposal may have inadvertently slipped out the CEO's attention, but his driver can salvage the whole situation by reminding him of the proposal. If the marketing 4P's is the only method you use to tackle every situation, chances are your method is not good enough to handle this one.

With a definite hierarchical structure, you wonder why there are still Left-Lefts you have to consider under the CEO who already has the highest power and authority. The fact is the CEO has to give due respect to his subordinates. Even when he sees your proposal as the most favourable for the company, he has to make sure he does not send out an image of doing micromanagement. The CEO can see you highly, but he will not want to find himself against the division head just because he wants to fight for you. You have to be aware of those Left-Lefts. If you do not grasp the whole idea behind "Left Circle of Left Circle", you find it very difficult to navigate through the web of influences to arrive at an eventual success.

Paying Attention to Every Left Circle in the Family

Moving on from the work environment to the family environment, we now use the case of wedding banquet to illustrate our theory. What is this huge setting of wedding banquet for? A wedding is for the bride and groom, naturally. Why does it become a matter of a lot more than two persons with a lavish banquet on offer? When the bride requests that the wedding should go with a banquet, she has her reasons. For the groom, the whole matter is all guided by the Left Circle. He will have to see if his Right Circle can satisfy the Left Circle demand. Even when he thinks it is unnecessary and wasteful, he cannot possibly deny the need of his most important Left Circle.

Who is influencing the bride's demand for holding a banquet? Very likely it is from her parents. They may see that it is important for their friends and relatives to witness their daughter's marriage. When her parents have this strong wish, the whole matter is out of the bride's hands. Even if her parents are not as demanding, the bride's sister may say, "I've done it. So, maybe she has to do it too." But the sister may just want the whole treatment to be no more and no less than hers: "I couldn't do this at my wedding. Why can she do it?" Little can the couple do to control the sister, but she does have influence. She may even have influence on where they hold the banquet because she compares everything. Not just the sister, influence may come from anyone including the relatives.

It may also happen that the groom's in-laws are apart in their views. When bride's mother pushes for the banquet, her father may extend a great deal of empathy: "Do you not care about your daughter's future? How come you ask them to spend all their money on a lavish banquet with no benefit to them?" If a conflict arises between the in-laws, the groom will come to a situation of "damned if you do and damned if you don't". He cannot take sides. His father-in-law's position may be more advantageous to him, but he cannot afford to ignore his mother-in-law, not a bit. This is a very complex situation to be in.

To the groom, apart from his wife's side, his own parents are also his Left Circle. What can the influences be? Certainly, the financial, social and cultural factors are in the consideration as far as the wedding goes. Suddenly, his parents may come up with a big idea: "Our neighbours Mr. and Mrs. Wong went along with their son on their honeymoon trip.

Don't you think we can do that as well?" Now, the neighbours have influence too. For all things in the world, they choose to follow what their neighbours do.

Combining all the demands from your Left Circle and your Left Circle of Left Circle, you can have many conflicting requests that you simply cannot satisfy at the same time. You cannot have a banquet and not have a banquet. You cannot hold the banquet in one place and also in another place. Your parents' side and your wife's parents' side both want their ideas to be your first priority. These issues are very confronting if they happen.

Real life has it that you can have many conflicting demands by your Left Circle and your Left-Left. Demands that go to the extremes are not solvable. Finding a consensus is difficult even for someone well conversant in Left-Right Circles. Family issues are usually more complicated than those at work because the worst-case scenario at work is that you quit. But you cannot choose your parents, your children, or even your closest relatives. The marketing methods that you use in the business world to solve problems have very limited effect in the family context. Conversely, if you have a good way in keeping your family affairs in very good shape and order, you can take it for use in the business context.

In the family case above, you may not be able to find a perfect solution, but extending your best understanding and best effort to find a balance will help. But beware of a possible change in your relationship with your Left Circle. If your fiancée understands you and is committed to you, then not only are you safe but you have a very strong ally working alongside you. However, should that trigger a doubt in your fiancée about your sincerity, the confidence your closest Left Circle has in you is shaken. You can expect more undesirable things to happen to you.

Handling of Family's Left Circle and Left-Left as in a Chinese Opera

Another example of a family feud is from the Chinese opera "The Arrogant Princess". It is a tale dating back to the Tang Dynasty where General Guo Ziyi was celebrating his birthday. His daughter-in-law was the Princess, who felt she should not condescend to a vassal even though the person was her father-in-law. Her refusal to pay respects got her husband Guo Ai ridiculed in front of other guests at the birthday banquet. In his fury, Guo Ai stormed back home and slapped his wife, the Princess. Pretending that she had been injured, the Princess went back making complaints to the Emperor. The Emperor of course loved his daughter, but he also knew how spoiled she was. He knew that his daughter was wrong not to pay her respects to her father-in-law. So, what should the Emperor do? Should he punish his son-in-law, the Prince Consort, because he hit the Princess?

Multiple versions of "The Arrogant Princess" are available. Here, we focus on the conclusion part which highlights how the Left Circle of Left Circle theory can be applied. Under this situation, who is the Left Circle of the Emperor? It has to be his beloved daughter. You would think that the Emperor would choose to punish the Prince Consort: "How dare you! Execute him!" For the Emperor, the country and the people are also his Left Circle, and his faithful and capable General Guo Ziyi is his very important Internal Left Circle. Does he want to punish the General's son? As the Emperor shouted out an order to execute the Prince Consort, the Princess was shocked and immediately begged her father to take the order back. Why? Was she not coming to complain about the abuse in the first place?

In fact, the Emperor's order was not intended for a real execution. He was skilfully using the Left Circle of Left Circle theory to find a way to resolve the matter. He knew the Princess did not want her husband to die. In fact, she loved him, only that she had a wilful character that made her constantly complain. Certainly, the Emperor was fully aware of that. The Emperor's Left Circle is the Princess, and the Princess's Left Circle is the Prince Consort. The Princess might have said that she wanted the Prince Consort punished, but her motive was just to whine. The Emperor did not want to kill the Left Circle of his Left Circle. He gave the execution order just to scare his daughter. He believed that it would make her change her mind and beg for revoking the order. The emperor understood his Left Circle, and used this understanding to deal with this Left Circle of Left Circle issue.

This example gives us an insight into the intertwining network of the Left Circle, which while bringing us a lot of intricate challenges, can be very useful in helping us solve a lot of problems. Our actions have to go beyond the fundamental concept of a Left Circle plus a Right Circle to the skilful use of the entire Left Circle and Left Circle of Left Circle network to establish our positioning. Mastery in the Left Circle of Left Circle concept can take us to the pinnacle of marketing and strategy.

Social Policies from a Network Viewpoint

Other than work and family, the Left Circle network has applications on the social aspect.

The government's Left Circle in an Assembly includes all members of the council. When the government wishes a certain policy or legislation passed, it needs to convince the council members to give their consenting votes. Who are the people influencing the council members? Leaders of the political parties? "Sponsors" of the parties or members? Authority figures and consultants in the parties and system? Public opinion? Or voters in the members' constituencies? The answer depends on many things, not least the political party, the political system, and the social structure and system, etc.

Now, we come back to what we first discussed in this chapter — Marketing 3.0. The Left Circle of Left Circle is important on the basis of Marketing 3.0, which emphasizes on an "ecosystem". That is, the industrial chain and all aspects of the social system. The Left Circle network is an intricate and intertwining one. Every person you come across can be one of your many Left Circles, or your Left Circle of Left Circle, or even your Left Circle of Left Circle of Left Circle. To a government official, his network is not restricted to the hundred or so council members in the Assembly. There are many views and positions in the entire network, and those are the many considerations you take that help you to make your positioning right.

In business, product and service providers cannot just focus on completing the transactions and then abandon the customers right after sales. This simplistic approach belongs to Marketing 1.0. At Marketing 3.0, the sight is set on the whole Left Circle network including all the interpersonal relationships therein. It is completely apt to apply this concept towards social policies. A good government should know the Left Circle of Left Circle and Marketing 3.0 concepts comprehensively and use them as the basis for their work to achieve long-term benefits of the whole society.

Summary

I hope the examples in this chapter would stimulate a thought in you about the way you conduct yourself in face of the many Left Circles and Left

Circles of Left Circle. To face the contradictions in all needs and demands, the key is in finding a balance. A decision needs to be made nevertheless, and all you can do is to make it with your best judgement, wait for the result, and then review it. If you do not see the matter from a Left Circle point of view, your decisions are bound to be wrong.

You need to find suitable positioning for yourself to handle your Left and Right Circles, and good relationships with your Left Circle and Left-Left are crucial. You cannot count on basic Marketing 1.0, using inconsistent approaches to deal with the situations to just get what you want, and ignore the consequences. It is very damaging if you do not stick with one set of principles.

I hope that after this chapter, when you deal with your Left Circle, you will rise above a sales and marketing approach to management, strategy, leadership, passion, compassion and life essence considerations. Your great character and broad wisdom will support you in this continuous effort to rise. You can do this because you embrace the concept and are capable in utilizing the Left Circle of Left Circle.

Chapter 7

Turning Left into Right: Turning Left Circle into Company's Strong Supporters to Increase its Strength

Strengthening Right Circle with Left Circle

This chapter discusses a very special concept: Turning Left Circle into Right Circle. Who are in the Left Circle? They are the people we need to satisfy. The very basic mode of interaction between the Left Circle and the Right Circle is that the customer pays for the product or service we provide. When we get our transaction done, we have realized Marketing 1.0. Then, if the customer is satisfied with the product or service, with both sides happy, it is Marketing 2.0. But this simple relationship is not enough to sustain, let alone develop, our businesses in this world. The world will not make much progress, or move very slowly, if we stay in this simple buy and sell model.

As the term suggests, "Turning Left Circle into Right Circle" is to utilize the people who we need to satisfy into people who would help us satisfy other people who we need to satisfy. This means that we let our Left Circle come and participate in improving our system. On the one hand, they pay us for the product so we can invest further. On the other hand, they give us a lot of information regarding the Left Circle, which we use to improve ourselves. Also, when they use our product, they are helping to demonstrate to other people how good our product is. This motivates our Internal Left Circle too, as our own people see the product that they make becomes popular.

To turn Left Circle into Right Circle, we have to transcend Marketing 2.0 and move up to Marketing 3.0, a level which is network-driven. Generally, people consider turning Left Circle into Right Circle as a good conversion in itself, but in fact, that is not powerful enough. The real change ought to be in turning Left Circle into Right Circle such that the whole system is enlarged.

The duty of marketing people is to manage a system, not to sell a product per se. This is the basic premise in turning Left Circle into Right Circle. In the system, we have all the Left Circles that we need to look after. The first group consists of the buyers who come to buy our products. Who are the users? Who are the ones who actually pay? We need to understand that relationship too. Then, we have colleagues that we need to look after as well. Our staff and our bosses are in our Internal Left Circle. Extending this concept out, our suppliers, our buyers, the society, the government and the environment are all our Left Circles. Understanding that we operate in this large system, having an ability to turn Left Circle into Right Circle will yield significant benefits.

While the customers have bought and used our product, they can feedback to us a lot of information about our product. In a narrower sense, this information will help our company to improve. In a broader sense, the information will benefit our system a lot. This is the central idea of turning Left Circle into Right Circle.

To discern such a complicated concept, we need a lot of practical examples. After going through the examples, we can come back to look at the basic concept above. You will learn to closely observe the behaviours of the various Left Circles (including their acceptance, usage and exchanges), and develop targeted methods to get your Left Circles to come around and do things that benefit your company. The many Left Circles that the company faces can now be put together in an effort to bring ongoing benefits to the company.

You have to overcome these first barriers to turn your Left Circles into Right Circle. Managing to do so is a pathway to success. Should you fail at this first hurdle, you will simply remain busy just staying afloat. You may want to make contributions to the world, but your contributions will be very limited, not the bold and powerful impact that you would like. To want to make a good impact, this chapter is an important learning tool for you.

First Level of Turning Left into Right: Word-of-Mouth

We start from the very first level of turning Left Circle into Right Circle. The very first level is to produce word-of-mouth. What does that mean? If a consumer buys your product and never talks about it again, you are not getting this important opportunity to promote your product. You might believe: "When you have musk, you will automatically have fragrance." But the reality is different. The significance of word-of-mouth is in the power of public opinion.

It is just the same product. But when you receive praises from the users giving their seal of approval, your product will be seen in a different light by the wider market. In marketing, we have a theory on promotion that is described as "know it, understand it, like it, do it, and get used to it." Word-of-mouth contributes importantly to the workings of this theory. Your product is being talked about, so people start to "know" it exists. Because it is talked about, people start to take steps to "understand" it. This knowledge and understanding will turn some people to "like" it. When they find your product good and affordable, they start to "do" what it takes to buy it, eventually leading them to "get used to" your product.

Many products face sluggish sales. Very often, the bottleneck to popularity is not that people do not like the product but that they lack a strong promotional push from the users to get it widely known. When you understand the importance of user recognition, you would make it a crucial element in your marketing plan.

The example is Apple's iPhone. An Apple trademark appears on every one of its products. People identify themselves deeply with the product through this trademark. But is it a blind faith? In fact, it can also be a reflection of people's confidence in the brand quality. Apple receives very good publicity. People see it as a very progressive company, delivering better and better versions of the product through various releases. This confidence makes people speak positively about the brand, giving it the all-important word-of-mouth. This advantage brings the company a much stronger Right Circle.

Another good example is Tesla which is a successful case of turning Left Circle into Right Circle. Tesla's users like to boast about their cars on social media a lot. Whenever possible, they take their cars out to show to other people. Some highlight their contribution to environmental causes, while others laud how quiet the car is. Approvals come from all sides, and the car establishes its positive image among car users and buyers. No change whatsoever has been made in the car, but the product is increasingly seen as a delight in people's minds.

Marketing has four important elements, called the marketing 4P's — Product, Price, Place (channels) and Promotion. Product and price are both important attributes — the product has to be able to serve the functional requirement of the users, and the price has to be set at an affordable level — but if the product is not supported by effective distribution channels and strong sales promotions, it will not get known and will not be made available to the buyers.

There are many excellent products in this world that unfortunately do not get known in the market. The product can be excellent in terms of its ability to satisfy the Left Circle, but the Left Circle has no way of knowing it. The Left Circle has no way to verify if it is a good or fitting product. Obviously, there is no way you can turn your Left Circle into Right Circle to help you, and you are stuck in your lower level of Left Circle theory understanding.

Word-of-mouth comes from a subjective view. When one has experience in the product and feels good about it, he will let others know, to the extent of propagating his view through various means. In some cases, it creates a big network effect, leading to hot discussions that create a rush for the product. Participants are unaware that they have joined in to create this network. This network is created from the simple word-to-mouth. It is just that when the scale gets larger and larger, it produces an enormous effect.

I use the example of Airbnb. Since Airbnb was first known, what has it gone through in order to become a household name with almost everybody having been its user? Perhaps Airbnb has itself advertised or appeared in newspaper reporting, but these deliberate promotions are far less effective than the actual users sharing their experiences. Better still is that the service has been used by some celebrities, and people will wonder, "Wow, even this superstar says it is good!" But if the superstar has actually received money from Airbnb, people will just take it as an advertisement, and its believability is hugely discounted.

To be convincing, praises have to come from the heart. It is not a paid service, and the feeling expressed needs to be genuine. Once such appreciations come on to the mass media and especially the social media these days, the effects will be magnified to create a full network. People will go online and talk about how many times they have used the service and what experience they have when staying in the accommodations.

The other example that is similar to Airbnb is Uber where a lot of users help to promote the service. Very often, what a stranger tells you fares far better in believability terms than the company tells you the same thing a hundred times. We trust the person because he is seen as objective, while the company is just taken more as self-praising. Particularly when you find it impossible that the person can be directly influenced by the company, you find credibility in the person speaking the truth. The person who says nice things about a company or a product forms with other like-minded people a network circulating word-of-mouth. They might conduct a conversation like this: "What an experience that you have! I also have this really incredible experience: I would have been in deep trouble if I didn't use Uber that time." It gets to the pinnacle of word-of-mouth.

Given the effect of word-of-mouth, some people add one step to the process of promotion: After we "know it, understand it, like it, do it, and get used to it", we "spread it". That is, your Left Circle is so satisfied with your product that it undertakes to "spread" good words about it. If your Left Circle does that for you, you have a superb marketing position. As a matter of semantics, we can include "spread it" into "get used to it": we can get used to buying as well as promoting the product.

Strictly speaking, "turning Left into Right" only happens when the Right Circle is able to satisfy the Left Circle. That is, there is an Area C where the Left Circle and the Right Circle overlap. The Left Circle is so happy with the Right Circle that it voluntarily does something to strengthen the Right Circle. But even so, you cannot ignore those criticisms that also exist in your Left Circle. As you wish to be more integrated with your Left Circle, you should proactively adjust your Right Circle just so that your Left Circle sees you in an even better light, such as when you improve your products and services or deliver a more reassuring message. While mostly positive, some messages can be negative circulating within the network. You have to respond to those criticisms correctly.

You cannot control what is circulating in the network. When good messages give you tremendous help, bad ones can cause you great damages as well. You cannot expect to lay your big hands on the network to try to control it as it is not controllable. The speed of circulation is very fast too. The key is to make sure that you do not do anything wrong. Should you make a mistake, just admit it and make amends. Even if 99%

of your users are satisfied, you do not expect all of them to speak out to support you. But if the 1% of users who are not satisfied set a scene and arouse big discontentment within the circle, you get a very unpleasant situation. Just be aware that "bad news travels a lot faster than good news".

Not only the Right Circle, sometimes even the Left Circle itself cannot control the negative word-of-mouth circulating in the network. Once a certain bad word has gone out, it can hardly be taken back. Even if an apology is made, such as issuing a correction statement "Sorry, what I said about that person was wrong", people barely pay attention to this non-sensation. But the original accusation of wrong-doing will never stop. There is no way you can retrieve the spilt water.

If the Left Circle firmly believes that you are in the wrong, then it is almost impossible that you can clear your bad name. Your word-of-mouth network supported by the social media today will spread your bad name fast and wide, and you will have to face up to the sanction. You need to understand the way the system works today and be cautious about everything you do even when you think you have done nothing wrong. The consequence can be dire.

In the old days, you could control the dissemination of your bad news to a certain degree through your money power or relationships with the press. It is not the same anymore. The difficulty with the online world today is that you have virtually no way to trace who is circulating the bad news about you. People do not have to use their real names. The person who circulates the news can face no bad consequence while you will suffer. David now has a lot of ways to upset Goliath. The newspapers may even take the online gossips and propagate them through their print and online machineries. The spread is wide and far. These days, should you not have vital knowledge in the online world, you are almost deemed unsuitable to run a business.

Second Level of Turning Left into Right: Co-creation

Up a level in this network effect is "Co-creation". How ingenious can co-creation be? It is intelligent and artful work because you cannot differentiate between whether the customer is coming to buy your product or whether he is there to work as your partner. The Left Circle appears to be doing your job, and this is definitely turning Left Circle into Right Circle.

Now, some of you may see that word-of-mouth is indeed a form of co-creation. Facebook is a common platform for such co-creation work. First of all, it allows for "re-creation". At the early stage of internet, it was all about distributing information. But more and more people start to interact with the information they have. This phenomenon continues to grow in size and form. Today, it is common that people take a picture online, re-create it into a parody or satire, and re-distribute it. The Left Circle uses this technique to re-disseminate information and share views and opinions, creating a strong influence on other people. The Left Circle has now developed into a much stronger power to influence through co-creation.

You can see all forms of co-creation in Facebook today. Take the case of the professor socializing with his friends on Facebook. When he sees his friend's post about a certain good deed of people, which was originally distributed for her friends, he can easily click on the "Share" button to re-post it as his own to share with more people. The work has now become a co-creation, and he has turned from a Left Circle of his friend to become her Right Circle.

Here we have to emphasize again that the prerequisite for "turning Left into Right" is that the Right Circle is able to satisfy the Left Circle, overlapping to form an Area C. If this does not happen, you cannot expect your Left Circle to come and strengthen your Right Circle. Just as we show in the Facebook example above, the professor has to like his friend's post before he re-posts it and shares it. He has to be impressed first before he is willing to co-create. There are people who like to "tag" someone else in their posts even though the post content has nothing to do with that person. This is to make the post available to his network of friends if his security and privacy setting is lax. This form of self-promotion without others' permission is not ethical. Neither has it obtained his approval nor has it got him happy with the content. In response, he should ignore the post and adjust his privacy and security setting to disallow this auto-sharing. He does not agree to co-create.

The social media enables many forms of turning Left into Right. The professor above is taking his friends on the social media as his Left Circle. At times he finds it difficult to understand the ways to set up his Facebook or WhatsApp account, and he has to take it on to the platform to consult his capable friends. This is the time when his turns his Left Circle into his

Right Circle (of course, this has to be subject to a very good relationship he has with his friends).

Then, there are situations where he can swap back as his friend's Left Circle. His friend wants to take the opportunity to ask him for advice in some of her matters. So, she sends him a message like this: "Professor, I have wanted to get in touch with you for a long time, but I don't want to bother you when you are busy. I certainly can do what you ask for, but can I come back to you afterwards for some advice from you on a couple of my matters?" Now, as his friend's Left Circle, he is turned into her Right Circle. With them having their respective needs, they are interchanging positions regularly. They are both happy as they blend together into a harmonious whole.

An Excellent Example of Left-Right Blending

At this point, we will use an excellent example to conclude our turning Left into Right discussion. The example is our EMBA programme.

To start an EMBA programme, the first thing to do is not to seek positive word-of-mouth. We need to first establish our "product" — our course content, teaching quality and learning environment. Every student who joins, he will be looked after and his requirement will be satisfied. We will see every student as a special case, and will pay attention to each case, at least until the student's career comes to an end. Should any student come back at any point to ask for assistance, we will do what it takes to help him. This is the basic 4P perspective in marketing to develop our product.

As we have a strong external network, we understand that a lot of prominent social figures are willing to co-create with us. This is a step for the Left Circle to turn into a Right Circle. We have to convince these guests to come to our EMBA class to talk to us, but they are still our Left Circle. We have to satisfy their needs, whether it be in the form of financial compensations or simply our utmost respect. When they come, they perform as our salespersons, helping us to promote our courses, in effect becoming our Right Circle. Most of them are happy to accept a symbolic level of compensation or take up the job as voluntary service. This helps to lower our cost and fee. Our Right Circle becomes even stronger. With these important contributions, we start to establish our reputation and positive word-of-mouth.

Next, we learn directly from our Left Circle — our students. Students give their feedback after class, helping us to know if the class is delivering what they want. There are all sorts of comments and requests coming: "Professor, can you adjust the schedule a bit? It clashes with another class." "The class is good. Can we have an extension class on the same subject next year?" "Can we have a class one month before the next school term to learn to do the report and have enough time to prepare for it?" We take these comments and do what we need to satisfy their requirements. Then, some other students turn around and ask: "Why do we have just one class this month and not any more until a month later?" We explain to them that this is what the students prior to them suggest.

This is how we learn from the students and make change and adjustment based on their feedback. This is like sustaining our ability for war through fighting the war. As we fight the war, we learn from the fight to improve our capability.

Students are more satisfied with the course quality as the course continues to improve, but students are also happy to see that their suggestions are well responded to. Their suggestions prompted us to cancel class for one subject after 10 years. Students feel e-commerce should no longer be a separate subject but should be a part of the digitalization process that comes under every subject. Also, we have started new functions and activities such as the EMBA Forum. Students feel that new concepts such Big Data, Internet of Things and FinTech have much new development every year, and they should not be "taught" but "discussed" through these forums. So, we suggest to them that they co-create with us: "Since you are so interested, we let you organize the forums for those subjects."

So, in that sense, are the students our Left Circle or our Right Circle? Before they start, they are the Left Circle. Right after they start, they are still the Left Circle with a level of loyalty not too high. But once their loyalty has elevated to the level where they feel they co-exist with the programme, face any problems together, and see success and failure as their own, then they are no different from our own Right Circle, just wanting the programme to improve as much as we do.

Now we are giving students the responsibility to organize the forums. We ask them to come up with three topics and then discuss with us to arrive at a common view. We would ask them, "How many speakers do you want for this forum? Which area do you think you still need some expertise?" They may say, "We need an expert on FinTech. Do you know anyone who is well regarded in this area?" Then, we ask again, "What are your concerns if we go for this area?" They say, "We fear the speaker may only have theory without practical hands-on experience." "Then what do you expect?", we ask. They suggest, "We have heard of Applied Science & Technology Research Institute (ASTRI). One of its groups is said to have created a simulation model that can be played like a game machine but can lead us through the workings of FinTech."

After these exchanges, we have found that we have a lecturer who is a director at ASTRI responsible for the model. He then comes to speak to our students at the forum.

This example demonstrates that as we develop word-of-mouth, we need to build a tightly knit people network. People do not see each other as different within the network where students can perform the role of the teachers, and vice versa. They all share the same values and purpose. They all want the school to be the best in the region for business education. They are setting the bar for the industry. But this high standard has to be achieved through a united effort. All need to blend together without differentiating between you and me. All are there to co-create and to push the boundaries as best we can.

While working to the best of our ability, we have to transcend ourselves and expand our limits. This is necessary because the world always moves ahead into new territories. To do this, we need to maintain a high-functioning people network. This network includes the students, teachers and alumni. As everyone in the network is interlinked and intertwined, it is difficult to distinguish between who is the Left Circle and who is the Right Circle. Everyone can be in the Left Circle, and everyone can be in the Right Circle.

The students are certainly our Left Circle because they pay school fees and they deserve to be satisfied. But satisfied as they are, can they be turned into our Right Circle to exert their power? How come students can participate in forums on blockchain, internet of things and O2O? Where do they get that knowledge from? These seem to be the things students can teach us better than we teach them. Most of the teachers can learn from the students instead. But can we teachers help them in the course of education? Of course, we can. Otherwise, we will not be standing on the podium talking about marketing, strategies, economics, or these sophisticated concepts. But we should never treat education as one-way teaching — it is much more like mutual learning.

If the concept of turning Left into Right is not used by schools and universities, all the teaching would be treated just as a transaction. Once the students graduate, the transaction is completed. When the transaction is done, the relationship is over. As the transaction brings you income, you have to deliver a product that the students want. But if you cannot deliver something that has a value exceeding what the students expect, they will not see your programme as outstanding. Eventually your product will dwindle and fade.

As a matter of necessity, you have to deliver a value that is in the order of 2–4 times of what the students expect. You often hear our EMBA students amazingly say, "This function I have attended is already worth the whole year's school fees." If such overjoy can sustain until the end, you will have a very happy alumnus. Some alumni told us, "Luckily I have learned the concept of net present value, and it helped me tremendously in a negotiation that saves my company a lot. I have wanted to tell you this for a long time, Professor, and now I have this chance to tell you face-to-face." Alumni are a special force in education. A lot of alumni hold very fond images of their alma mater.

If students have developed loyalty towards the school, continuing until their graduation, they would become a super strong Right Circle for the school as alumni. One of the very important contributions of alumni is recommending the school to others. The effect of alumni giving recommendation is much stronger than the Right Circle doing it itself. As the programme administrators, people know that we will not speak badly about our own programme. But when the alumnus speaks, his credibility is much higher.

Can alumni help the students? Of course, they can. Alumni can offer a big helping hand when students seek advice for a report or find sponsors for their functions. When students and other alumni plan for an IPO, they can possibly get all the professional support needed from the alumni network, including lawyers, accountants, investment bankers, underwriters and sponsors. There are a lot of real-life cases that have benefited from this network. What makes all these possible are the intimacy and sense of belonging that have developed within the group, many a time complemented by the professor acting as go-between.

We have two alumni, one in our class 10 years ago, the other 20 years ago. They were our Left Circles in school. As we see them subsequently earning public recognition and fame, we have an immense feeling of comfort and joy. At a certain point, we decided that we should invite them back to the university to speak to the current students. At that point, they were still our Left Circles, and we had to use our Right Circle power to persuade them to come. We wrote letters to them giving them a reminder that we had good times during their days with our university, hoping that such memories arouse emotions that spur them on to accept a visit back at the alma mater.

We know what kind of persons these alumni are. It is easier in that way to make them our Right Circle. We liaised with the two alumni above for some time, and they finally agreed to come and share their experiences with our students. The students responded well to their speeches and found their practical experiences support the theories that they learned. The event was a great success. These kinds of activities are a great help to develop an advantage for us. Coming as guest speakers, our alumni have turned from being our Left Circle to become our Right Circle.

As an educational institution, we have to maintain excellent relationships with our students and alumni. We can harness our students' and alumni's powers to help us bolster our strengths. The full integration of these strengths and powers will take us to the summit of our excellent practice: turning Left Circle into Right Circle.

Chapter 8

Unrecognized Needs: Exploring Unstated Needs, Satisfying Deeper and Higher-Level Needs

We have touched upon the idea of unrecognized needs in our previous chapters, but we have not discussed it in depth. We will go through a few examples in this chapter to elaborate it further.

What Are the Unrecognized Needs for a Restaurant?

Before we talk about "unrecognized needs", let us start from the exact opposite — "stated needs". The Left Circle has customers who find themselves having some needs, and they go to find companies that can provide products for their needs. Yet, even when their needs are so clearly defined, they do not find anyone having a matching product. From a marketing point of view, it is a sad state of affairs. There have been countless examples of this failure in satisfying clearly stated needs, not to mention the unrecognized needs that are not stated.

For restaurants, the first condition they have to satisfy is that the product has to be what they say it is — that is, with real ingredients. The second condition is that the food is safe. Will customers get sick after eating the food? After the first two, the third condition is nutrition — which is what food is all about. Are these "unrecognized needs"? Not at all. They are just very basic and clear needs from the customers.

But still there exist businesses who may go to the extent of using substandard ingredients to serve customers, believing that they will get away as long as they do not cause sickness. This definitely cannot satisfy the Left Circle even when a transaction is done. The Left Circle will move away. Some providers even use artificial ingredients in place of real ones. While by luck they may escape sanction by law, their behaviour is indeed cheating. That cannot satisfy even the very basic need, and there is no talk of any Left-Right Circles interaction. As a business, you have to first look at whether you are satisfying the "stated needs" before you can ever start thinking about "unrecognized needs".

Say, your restaurant is now able to use ingredients matching your promise, handle food as cleanly and hygienically as required, and deliver food that has good nutrition value, do you think you are satisfying all customer needs? What about the service levels? Do you treat your customers politely and with respect? Do you respond to customer requests quickly and accurately? Do you offer extra services when requested? Then, there is also a matter of comfort. Is the restaurant setting and décor pleasing to the customers. Are your facilities well maintained? Especially the toilets, are they giving customers a good feeling of cleanliness? Does your total environment give customers a good sense of confidence, which has to include good behaviours in your kitchen behind the scenes?

Are the above "stated needs" or "unrecognized needs"? Perhaps customers are not as explicit in stating what they expect before they come to your restaurant, at least not to such details, but these are definitely questions you have to think about.

What kind of result do you expect to see when these issues are not carefully thought through? Not too many customers would like to come back when they feel they are not respected, no matter how good the food is. If you squeeze in extra tables and put people very close together, many customers would not be happy. Customers certainly do not want to be disturbed by conversations going around at neighbouring tables, especially if those are loud and rude talks, or kids are seen being roughly treated. All those are needs definitely, even though rarely would customers have them as clearly specified when they choose a restaurant.

Restaurants should give serious thoughts to the above and other needs. Their considerations should include aspects such as space (if high ceiling is possible) and sceneries and views outside (greeneries or packed buildings), which can add to customers' delight and pleasure. What kinds of needs are these — "recognized needs" or "unrecognized needs"? Whichever they are, a restaurant should have all of these aspects carefully thought through during planning. (*Note*: the needs discussed above are generalized ones, without pointing to any specific persons.)

Adding to these considerations is the time factor. While food can be excellent in a lot of restaurants, the long waiting time to get in is a hindrance. In some restaurants, even after you have reserved your table, you still have to wait some considerable time. If without reservation, there is no hope of getting in when just showing up. If a restaurant insists on accepting customers only with reservations, then it is shutting out all walk-ins. If customers with reservation do not turn up, what can they do with the empty tables? Then, if the restaurant allows queueing, it has to ensure it runs a fair system, without allowing queue-jumping happening always as special cases.

When issues like booking and waiting have nothing to do with the food, it is part of the total feeling that affects customer perceptions. Customers come to the restaurant not only for food. They seek enjoyment for the time they spend there. Needs associated with this expectation have to be fully comprehended.

The basic needs of customers are to fill up, to have hygienic food, and perhaps a bit more demanding, to be respected in a restaurant. There are all sorts of other needs by different people based on who they are and what they want for different occasions. Some need a very pleasant environment. As long as those demands are reasonable and non-intrusive to other people, they have every freedom to want to have them. We cannot criticize someone for spending too much, such as to say, "Wow, you can get a good meal here for $3, but you choose to go there to spend $30. Why do you want to spend that money?" What exactly does he want by spending that much? Maybe he is trying to please his respected teacher back in a place where warm feelings can be enjoyed again since they were there 30 years ago.

This customer's need is "to take his teacher to a nice place for dinner". To be the restaurant they want, it has to have the warm atmosphere. The environment has to be quiet and cosy so as to produce this warm atmosphere. The exact image of this warm atmosphere is not something that the customer can visualize and clearly spell out himself. This is therefore an "unrecognized need". Patrons often come to the restaurant just wanting to have a good time with their friends and relatives, and food is a secondary need. People should go for higher needs over and above basic needs to attain greater value for their lives.

Why do people go to a specific restaurant? Possibly because the restaurant has done something extra that the customers want but did not realize prior. Customers can only realize it is what they want when they experience it. Vegetarians go to vegetarian restaurants for known reasons of health, environmental protection and kindness to animals. But they do not expect that they can meet up with like-minded people there. They find people on their wavelength, and such relationships give them the reason for going back again and again. In this case, their "unrecognized need" is satisfied before they realize it.

Unrecognized Needs for Libraries

You go to a library to search a book or read a book. But do you recognize that the library is a place more than for storing books? Libraries in fact attract like-minded people to go there. They may not talk with each other, but they feel their co-existence. Every day you see a certain senior citizen there reading newspapers, but one day he does not show up, and you have some uneasy feeling. "Where has that man gone?" you wonder. Luckily, he comes back in an hour, and you feel relieved. Such a sentiment has nothing to do with the books, but it has developed in you, giving you quite a different meaning in life. Only if you look back carefully into your day's work would you find this an "unrecognized need" of yours. This subtle need transcends physical, physiological and security needs into the higher-level needs of belonging, love and care, or even self-identity.

"Knowledge discovery" is another high-level need. Why is this an "unrecognized need"? Most of the information that is circulated around, particularly in on our daily social media conversations, is at best superficial and aims more at grandstanding. To get an essential understanding in our deep-down quests for spirituality, love and ideal society, we need to "come across" good books in libraries to trigger our discovery process. This is one of the many "unrecognized needs" that we have related to libraries.

Unstated Needs by Taxi Customers

We turn to the taxis now, and this is an area where we can clearly demonstrate what we mean by "unrecognized needs".

Now, I am in a taxi wanting to go from Wanchai to the Chinese University in Shatin. Among all the options, why do I decide to take the taxi? My journey is my "stated need", and I have made some estimates of the time required by each transportation mode. All are stated needs.

The first thing the driver tells me is that at this time of the day there must be heavy traffic through the Lion Rock Tunnel and suggests that we detour via the Tate's Cairn Tunnel. We travel around the city almost every day, so we understand what the traffic condition is like. But since the driver has already said so, I would feel hesitant to insist on the original route, lest he would get his displeasure known through some unpleasant behaviour. If we are hit with a standstill traffic condition after we insist, then the driver may counter back, saying. "I told you so!"

Taking a taxi, I want to get to the destination fast and do not want to be stuck in the traffic. But when the driver suggests taking another route, is he intending to satisfy my need? What other motives does he have making such a suggestion? Does he want to collect a higher fee, or does he really think of my need of wanting to be there on-time? If he really puts my interest first, why did he not give me more information so that I can be more assured? Perhaps he can say, "There is an accident somewhere over there, and the road has been very congested. If you don't mind, can I take a different route to avoid the trouble spot?" I will be more satisfied and willing to follow his suggestion if he gives that explanation. Drivers do not usually explain the road condition, but if he is Left Circle guided and willing to take an extra step to serve, I would have my "unrecognized need" very well satisfied.

Most of the time, we take taxis because we want to be fast. But is it just about being fast? We may also want a quiet, comfortable and hassle-free journey. But when we get into the car, the only need we can speak clearly out is where we want to go. The other needs remain unstated. Furthermore, not everyone can tell what it means by comfortable. Even when we say we want to be comfortable, we do not know as much as the driver on how to make it happen inside his car.

When the customers cannot spell out their "unrecognized needs", is it that there is no need for the driver to do something to satisfy them? Of course, the driver has to satisfy all needs to be good to the customers. If the driver follows our "Left Circle guided" principle in Chapter 2 to figure out all the needs of the passengers (stated or not), he will do his best to serve all those needs including the "unrecognized needs". The customers will find their expectation exceeded when their unrecognized needs are also taken up and satisfied.

Many drivers are unable even to fulfil the very basic requirement in the "Left Circle guided" approach. All the passengers see are their stern faces, even grumbles, without a single trace of courtesy that the customers expect as part of their stated needs. We hope to see taxi drivers being "Left Circle guided" so that they can think through what to do to satisfy stated and unrecognized needs of customers.

This is not difficult. When the passenger gets in the car and the driver sees that he starts to have his eyes closed, then he should refrain from any attempts to talk or allowing his equipment to make loud noises. The driver can also drive his car more steadily without making abrupt acceleration or braking. If the passenger has made it explicit that he wishes to be at the destination by a certain time, the driver has to make this his objective too (within the driving regulations). The driver can ask, "It will be a bit tight following the current route. Shall I switch to another route to make it faster?"

If the driver can be as considerate as this, then he is truly Left Circle guided. He can be sure of trust and understanding from his customers bringing about mutual satisfaction and harmony. His Right Circle can surely become ever stronger as he shows his understanding and capacity in satisfying "unrecognized needs".

What Needs Are Not Stated by Students?

How should the teacher teach in class? Should it be by just following the syllabus and making sure students get A or B in exams? What this approach can do is to satisfy only "recognized needs". Teachers can do more than that. If a teacher is late for class, what image does it portray? Students may follow suit and do not see it a problem to be late. If the teacher does not apologize and makes no attempt to explain why he is late, then it would create an even worse situation. Further, if the teacher habitually comes to class unprepared, not in his best form or displaying an authoritarian teaching style, this is all negative which makes him a very bad role model. Even when not all students ask for good role modelling, teachers have to be wary of bad influences.

Some teachers do exactly the opposite. Whatever the students want, they comply. Are they good teachers doing this way? Not necessarily. By doing so, the teachers may not be satisfying the real needs of the students because the students may not know what they need. We have a typical example: Whenever we start a school term, we would ask the students what they expect. The students reply, "Less homework. No exams." Some others say, "It is very difficult to do group projects. Difficult to get the people." Somehow, they are countered by other students: "If we do all individual assignments, we won't be having any interactions." Yet, some others ask, "Can we not do study reports?" Then, again there is a disagreement: "We can't learn if we don't do reports. We are here to learn."

If we let students take charge, they would name all different requirements, all being their "stated needs". But their needs can be without any consistency, and to follow every one of them, it creates a great deal of contradictions. It is very difficult for us to find our place and position. Are all these their real needs? We have to answer this question tracing back to our social responsibilities as teachers. Our purpose is to develop capable and responsible next generation for society. We want them to be duty-bound, honest, serious, while also full of interest and curiosity. We want them to be respectful of other people. This is what we need to consider to be good teachers.

In fact, students have a lot of "unrecognized needs". They are young, and they may not know what they are expected of by their teachers, parents, and society at large. We expect our students to outshine and outperform us. We want them to be the future leaders, pioneering their way into the future. Our expectations can be the guiding principles for them to develop. These could be their "unrecognized needs".

As such, can we allow them to get muddled in the way forward? Can we allow them to do half-work and get hazy understanding of the materials taught? If we do not reinforce teaching with assignments, we are unable to ascertain their level of understanding. If we do not give them group projects, they are unable to learn from others. At times, the most influential teaching is not from us the professors but from their seniors and teaching assistants. Students also learn from each other through their joint efforts. If we do not let them come into this environment, they cannot acquire the experience of working in this mode. We may tell them, "Listen to what I teach, come and do the exams afterwards, pass them, and you'll be fine." But that is not the way their needs can be satisfied.

By definition, students cannot state what their "unrecognized needs" are. As teachers, if we cannot discover their unrecognized needs, we would need a great deal to work on to become top-class teachers. Teachers should have knowledge of what the students need before they are able to tell them. Home assignments are what the students need to help them solidify their learning. But if the volume of assignments exceeds what they can afford, then it would produce a negative and discouraging effect. "Less assignments" is their stated need, and if we show an arrogant approach to ignore it altogether, they do not see us as working towards satisfying their needs. Needs can be contradictory, and the key lies in a balance. Assignments should be neither too much nor too little. Equally, they should be neither too hard nor too easy.

Apart from the assignments, lectures are another important teaching tool. Teachers should use a step-by-step approach to take students into a learning mode suitable to them. Progress needs to be assessed and adjustments made accordingly. We cannot insist on a fixed format and schedule for the course; it should be subject to learning progress. Your PowerPoint slides are there to assist understanding, and we cannot just read from the texts to teach, or else a recorded lecture would be just as good. When we are there, we have a role to interact with the students to enhance understanding.

Teachers are definitely role models, and this is just another "unrecognized need". Think about this: How many times have you decided how to do certain things because you have seen your bosses do it that way, or a good teacher of yours use a specific method, or some of your seniors practise certain kind deeds. All these are your role models. We do constantly learn from our leaders in society. We look at how they approach problems. We see how they embrace the five virtues "Humanity, Justice, Propriety, Wisdom and Credibility" in their problem-solving. Why do we have to consider those virtues even for a physics class? Because it is part of what the students need.

Case Study: Shaw College, CUHK

As we are with students, we are going to use two practical cases in education to explain "unrecognized needs".

Our first case is the Shaw College of the Chinese University of Hong Kong. As students come to the College, they are to receive professional and career training, and they would choose a major. The College has a fundamental objective, as set forth in the College motto "Cultivate Virtue, Go Deep in Learning". It is to urge students to first cultivate their virtue before going deep in learning. It also means that even if they are brilliantly capable but lack character and virtue, the College would not regard them as up to its standard.

If you ask the new students who come in, they are probably unaware that university education requires that they develop good character and social responsibility, and be trained to become leaders of their generation. During their time at the university, they are also indoctrinated not to go for self-serving pursuits but instead contribute to social good and progress. The education will address these "unrecognized needs" of the students.

Harvard professor Harry Lewis has written a book entitled *Excellence Without a Soul*. Having read the book, the former Head of Shaw College Professor Joseph Sung gathered a number of people of great insight and decided to do something around this idea. Altering it to project positivity, they adapted the book title for use as the College slogan: "Excellence with a soul, Leadership with a heart". This calls for a heart from all leaderships, executing from a soul in all excellent endeavours. With this purpose, the College also adopted the "Five Pillars" as directions guiding students to develop as great citizens of society. The Five Pillars could well be the solution to the "unrecognized needs" for the students.

The first of the Five Pillars is Nurturing Moral Character. Many would say, "I come to the university to train for getting a good job in the future. I need to learn the skills. Just let me get on with it and find a good job later!" But we believe they have "unrecognized needs". They need to learn to be sincere and righteous. We have to instil in them this concept.

When a person is sincere and righteous, equipped with relevant skills, he is ready for society. But he also has to be cautioned: "While learning the ropes, he needs to bide time but learn hard. Once declared good and ready, he can just wait in the wings and fly high upon an opportunity (although continuous learning is still a must)." To allow students to discover their own "unrecognized needs", we first instil in them the idea of sincerity and righteousness with a purpose to serve society.

The second pillar is Serving the Community. How do we make students recognize the importance of serving the community? What do they think would happen when they finish high school and come into university? They may think, "Wow, I am free from the shackles of high school rules and disciplines! The sky is now boundless." Well, boundless as the sky may be for a while before they have to get back to their learning disciplines.

Why do students study hard? Just for getting into university? Public exams are such a hassle in terms of the organization work. Why do people put in such enormous efforts into organizing those exams? Assessment aside, they want students to go for achievements that would eventually benefit the community. If teachers treat exams literally without referring back to the purpose, it is no different from a doctor taking the patient's temperature without treating the ailment that shows. People could be just doing a superficial job running exams simply for getting the scores.

What if a student gets the highest scores but does bad deeds? Why did the Harvard professor write this book *Excellence Without a Soul*? For him, he saw too many of his students being very talented people but ending up behind bars. He laments, "How come these students coming out of a Harvard education could end up being locked up? What have I done wrong as the College Dean?" To him, this is simply heart-breaking.

One needs to conduct oneself correctly before one can put order in one's family. Here, "family" can broadly represent a wider social group or community. That is, we need to be righteous to serve our community. Teachers have a duty to open up students' minds on these issues. Why should you be good to your "family"? If those elements towards social good are lacking in teaching, what students get are just technicalities in science, literature or sociology. The social element is not there.

As students, one has to be reasonably good academically to get jobs in the government, consulting firms or investment banks. But is it good enough to just see them in these organizations? Have we really satisfied our students' needs? Of course, by the very nature of "unrecognized needs", students do not come to us and tell us that they want to serve the community. Whenever we touch upon "unrecognized needs", we have to proactively reach out to guide those orientations and thoughts. When we start out, students may question: "I come here to study my subjects. Professor, why do you want us to learn all these broad principles about life?" So, it really counts on us to have the requisite skills to guide the students without being felt that those principles are being forced fed into them.

Doing this, we need to hold our moral straight all the time. We are not here to take the students to any harmful endeavours. As teachers, we only hope that our students achieve their life purposes reflected in their roles within the social networks and their readiness as a useful resource for society. "Understanding their life purposes" is indeed another "unrecognized need". If we ask the students, they cannot tell us about this need. We have to proactively work to unleash the positive energy that they have and start off a drive that sees them making great contributions to the community.

The third pillar is Caring for Motherland. By "Motherland", we mean the country of the student concerned. To care for the country, the first thing is to know about the country. To know, you have to learn and extend an empathy towards it. You would not know the country well if you do not learn and take in relevant information. You would not know what and where to help if you do not know how the country is doing. You may have areas where you want your country to improve, but you do not know where to set your hand to. You may have comments and criticisms about your country, but make sure you have your facts right. You make it right by learning and understanding.

Care is another matter. To care, you can borrow from the concept that we have learned. That is, to "know it, understand it, like it, do it, and get used to it". First, as we said, you have to know and understand it. Then, you like it, which does not necessarily mean you have to accept everything as it is today. You can think about how to change it as well. Without all the reformers, scholars and thinkers to change things over the years, our societies may not be as multi-dimensional as they are today.

What is the fourth pillar? Teachers' guidance is paramount for students to recognize this need. It is Developing Global Perspective. Teachers will guide students to broaden their views, help them step out of their own confines and take the world in their hands. Some students may ask, "Can I be that great?" As teachers, we can give a response like this: "There are countless people in history who have immense influence on the world. Say, Mother Teresa. What have you learned from her? Or, Nelson Mandela. He was put in jail for many years, and yet his influence was colossal. He might not have thought about that influence then, but ultimately he brought a new concept to the world!"

Students are definitely not spared the situations of facing people that are selfish, egoistic, self-centred, arrogant and bullying. They need to learn how to deal with those situations. On the issue of facing the world, they may have thought about their purpose and standing. Those may be their "recognized needs" already. As teachers, how do we understand what the students need? Do they still have "unrecognized needs" that we can help them with understanding? Students need to develop a global perspective. They need to open up their mind and take in new angles to look at the world. Not only will their "unrecognized needs" be satisfied but this new culture may take them to solving important problems in the world.

What is the fifth pillar? The commonly used term is Protecting the Environment. More precisely, it is Respecting the Environment. "Respect" is of a higher order than "Protect". Yet, even just on protection, there is a lot that needs to be done.

Many people want bigger houses, more furniture and material things, more helpers and many people to work for them. They compare cars and houses, and chase after bigger numbers over and above their friends and social peers. They live in a material world, obsessed with possessing and showing off their wealth. They care little about how their possessions and consumption have caused irreversible damages to the world.

Negligence towards the environment is commonplace among people by their habits and practices. It goes to every sphere of life. For example, for someone who always travels out for work, he may think that bringing a new set of toys back every time for his child is a compensation for the time lost. Irrespective of whether this is indeed a way to satisfy his kid (perhaps his kid treasures his time much more), the materials are wasteful of our natural resources and damaging against our natural environment. The damages are getting more and more severe, day by day and year by year. Environmental protection is an "unrecognized need" for a lot of people. People who respect the environment find joy and satisfaction in the work they do to protect and preserve it.

Teachers can impart concepts about environmental protection and inspire students to find their ways to contribute. The whole subject of environmental protection can be seen as opposing consumption, but people do need to look after their life essentials as well as medical, educational, and entertainment needs. Ultimately there ought to be a balance rather than a single direction dominating the agenda.

For example, do we need beauty services? Some would say it is unnecessary, but we cannot tar everybody with the same brush to denigrate all. What we can do perhaps is to promote inner beauty above outer beauty instead of campaigning to have all cosmetic products banned. We all have hobbies and interests, and if someone likes her beautiful look to give her self-confidence, then it is all legitimate as long as it goes without excesses.

Some people in the market feel they want cosmetics to help them look better. From a marketing point of view, that want produces a need, and that need produces some opportunities. A more creative way to serve this need would be to develop completely natural and environment-friendly beauty products. This is far better than prohibiting cosmetics. The success lies in whether you can convince consumers to go for a solution that satisfies both demands. Should any of our Shaw College students take this approach as her objective, we dare say we have done our job.

Educators are keen to teach children human virtues. Whether it is kindness, righteousness, integrity, respect or loyalty, they should be characteristics everyone embraces. To the students, these are probably their "unrecognized needs", and we as teachers should put our best effort in to enlighten them. An environment conducive to imparting these values on to the students should be one the College works towards developing, so as to enable these "unrecognized needs" to be realized.

The "Five Pillars" above helps to nurture such an environment. As students learn life skills and professional competences in the College, we can also help to realize their "unrecognized needs". Students take on these superlative values to guide them through their lives. Life is not about money-making, and the pursuit of higher meanings will enrich the life of every one of us.

Case Study: CUHK EMBA

The last case in this chapter about "unrecognized needs" is also about the CUHK. This time it is the EMBA programme.

The Shaw College has "Five Pillars", whereas the EMBA programme has "Six Pillars". The first and second pillars are the "recognized needs".

The first pillar is "Theory", which concerns how to manage your business and people, how to develop your strategies, how to identify your customer groups, how to use your own competences, how to integrate the Left and Right Circles to become your Area C, and how to nurture an Area D to serve your customers better and develop new customer bases.

As students learn the theories, they also need to know the practices. As a result, the second pillar is "Practices", which points to whether the theories learned are practical and can be applied as day-to-day business activities in the context of exercising leadership, management and strategic development.

These two pillars are what the students know why they are coming to the programme — their "recognized needs" *per se*. This is the foundation. If we cannot satisfy these needs, we are not in a position to talk about meeting the "unrecognized needs".

The next step is to help someone develop as a leader. This is what the third pillar "Internal Network" is all about. This gives a favourable environment to students so they can develop partnerships and friendships, much as they build a family. They will work together to develop new and better ideas to serve the business sector and general society. Using a "group of three" concept, we find that any combination of people has someone we can learn from. The partnership between people can create brilliant sparks and inspirations.

"Is this an 'unrecognized need'?" people would ask. Yes, it is. This is what the programme wants to do to nurture future leaders, which is one of our major aims. Staying in the first two pillars unfortunately would only take us that far. Not only should these ideas be used in education, they should be applied in any industry and in any capacity, just as we should all rise above our basic needs.

The fourth pillar is 'External Network'. The programme continuously takes in information, people networks and valuable resources from external sources. These useful resources are integrated in the programme to encourage students and alumni alike to interact with one another and produce positive results. What we encourage is not only doing business wisely but more in developing synergy between people to make greater things happen that moves the world forward. We want our people to get ahead to anticipate what will happen and pioneer in that direction. That is the model our EMBA programme operates on.

"External Network" shares our "group of three" concept. The idea is not to pursue self-interest and seek dominance over others. It is to make use of everybody's strengths and advantages so that they cooperate to bring common good to the group and community. Both Internal and External Networks are extremely important. Without the Internet Networks, students develop no friends. Without the External Networks, students are confined within and do not have reach outside that makes for success. If our programme does not provide the opportunities for both networks, we are not in the job of satisfying the "unrecognized needs" of the students.

The fifth pillar is "Strategic Perspective". All students in one way or another are aware they have to establish perspectives. But most may restrict their views to what the first two pillars prescribe. A person with real perspective can see what other people cannot, going from the surface to the structural level of problems and making effective long-term changes. By integrating ideas from Pillars 1–4, students can establish a perfect position to tackle core issues.

What we want today are leaders who can exercise keen observations, anticipate events and find the keys to solving very complex matters. When two countries contend for prominence, should their respective military and financial powers the determining factor of who wins? What does it mean by winning anyway? In ancient China, when Zhuge Liang (chancellor and regent of the state of Shu Han during the Three Kingdoms period) captured Meng Huo (rebel leader of the southern region) seven times, is that winning by definition? Why did Zhuge capture and release Meng seven times? Could he just get rid of him on the first capture?

The real objective of Zhuge was to make peace with the southern region. He wanted to co-exist with the region but not be bothered with their threats. He never intended to exterminate the region, which in a way was also impossible. By releasing Meng seven times, his intention was made clear to his opponents who finally acknowledged it by accepting friendships and alliances. If Zhuge took the initiative to just kill and destroy, the problem would never be solved.

When you block a flood at a certain point, it only diverts the water without solving the problem. The only way is to get to the source of the problem and clear the main obstacles. To solve those problems, you need a perspective and a problem-solving mindset. Students come in our programme with quite different perspectives from what we expect them to have. We help them to establish much broader ones during the course, all aiming to satisfy their "unrecognized needs".

The sixth and final pillar is "Social Contribution". At the first sight, perhaps you would say this pillar has nothing to do with the EMBA programme. But after reading this chapter, you should understand that if we do not set our programme to bring benefits to the community, we are not nurturing excellent young leaders. If we think we need only to satisfy what the students explicitly ask for after they pay us the fees, we are failing our purpose and expectation of society for not bringing them to become useful social assets.

Some business people look only at one side of the equation and take shortcuts to get things done. They may make work easy by skipping quality control, use substandard materials that are harmful to health and the environment, and engage illegal workforce or even child labour to achieve their purposes. When we run our programme, we cannot allow this to happen. We cannot allow our students to take the attitude that it is all about selling without caring about the consequences. This is what the sixth pillar aims to do: to eradicate selfish attitudes and stop producing students that are "excellent without a soul". This is how we want our programme to be truly excellent.

EMBA graduates will come out equipped with knowledge and intelligence to run businesses. This is all fine until someone deviates from his first aim. Should that happen, it is the failure of the course, because too much concentration has been placed on Pillars 1 and 2. A good course would put good-natured people together to establish links and connections (Pillar 3). To the outside, we encourage students to deploy and support good conscience in running business (Pillars 4, 5 and 6). These should all be their needs. But even when students do not realize this first and make no requests, as lecturers, programme directors and university leadership, we should take these on board ourselves, else we are not doing our job well.

Summary

Whether in education or in any other industry, if we seek only to satisfy the needs that are stated and care not about doing more to add value to the Left Circle, we are only doing basic low-level work. It does not truly satisfy the Left Circle needs. A situation like this can mean we have a fragile relationship with the Left Circle, or we are vulnerable to the Left Circle leaving once a better choice is available, or in the worst case, we are causing harm to our society. We hope by reading this chapter you get a good understanding of what it means by "unrecognized needs" and why they are so important.

Chapter 9

Seemingly Unrelated Left Circle: Exploring Non-apparent Left Circle for Better Results

Some Left Circles Are Invisible to You

This chapter discusses "seemingly unrelated Left Circle", which is a very important subject. For sustained development of our business, we need to improve on a continuous basis. We need to achieve ever higher effectiveness and efficiency, and deliver ever more personal services to our customers. To be at the very top, we even have to venture into completely new arenas.

When we do strategic planning, we usually put our focus on the Left Circle that is the closest and most obvious to us. This is certainly very important. There are things that this Left Circle explicitly asks for, and we have to deliver. There are other needs that this Left Circle has not yet recognized themselves, but we have to do our best to identify them and adjust our Right Circle to satisfy them. Other than the above, we also have our Internal Left Circle. As we build our business, we have to care about our own team by understanding their needs.

We have also covered the Left Circle of our Left Circle, and looked at who are the people influencing what our Left Circle needs. But what we have talked about are those Left Circles that can be easily seen. In this chapter, we will go deeper to look those Left Circles (including Left Circles of our Left Circle) that may not be seen or known, seemingly non-existent. These Left Circles (and Left Circles of our Left Circle) may not even know they have influence on somebody else. This type of Left Circle is called "seemingly unrelated Left Circle".

The Media and Organ Donation

Sometime ago, a mother in our community desperately needed a liver transplant, but she could not get a suitable one from the small number of donors in Hong Kong. Her daughter wanted to give a part of her organ to her mother, but she was barred from doing so being underaged as an organ donor. As the daughter was bitterly disappointed, the news was picked up by the media. The reporting attracted widespread attention in the community. No public appeal was made by the media for a donor though, and they were just reflecting the daughter's wish for allowing this special case to go through by some relaxation of the age limit so that she could give her mother a lifeline. What everyone had not thought of was that the reporting prompted a kind young lady who came forward and volunteered part of her liver for the sick mother.

The family was finding themselves helpless. They required a suitable organ for the sick mother but had no idea how to make their desperate situation known to others. Firstly, they had no idea who to appeal to. Secondly, they could not construct such a sensational story to get the due attention. The media played the critical role of a "seemingly unrelated Left Circle" just by doing their job.

The media were simply doing their job, picking up a story that they thought was news worthy. They did not intend to play the role as the invisible Left Circle — only that the story of the family itself had satisfied their need of news reporting. Their intention was different from the family's. But the role they inadvertently played as an invisible Left Circle was extremely important, which brought about a critical result. Had the media not reported the story, the kind lady as the Left Circle had no way of knowing such a situation existed, and the whole story would have been very different.

Seniors at Theme Parks

Oftentimes, we just scratch at the surface, and can hardly grasp the key issue behind what customers need. Theme parks are a classic example. As the name tells us, theme parks carry themes. The Ocean Park is about the ocean, and the Disneyland Park is about its cartoon characters. People go there to enjoy games and activities in the parks. These visitors are the most visible and obvious Left Circle, and what you need to do is to set your Right Circle to meet those needs.

In addition, you would respond to their additional needs when you identify them. These responses are according to the basic Left-Right Circles principles. Say, the theme parks are often visited by the whole family, and there are various needs from different age groups. As the young go for the activities, there need to be facilities for the old, who come simply for the enjoyment of being with the family. With restaurants and resting areas, the park looks after the extended needs of the Left Circle, but still these are not the "seemingly unrelated Left Circle" we wish to talk about.

Are all needs in the Left Circle being satisfied by those facilities? Not at all. The fact is that incomes of theme parks come not only from entrance fees but also from the souvenir shops. The seniors who do not go to the machines need places to kill their time. They would visit the souvenir shops and often have those thoughts and conversations: "Would our grandkids like this stuff? If not our grandson, maybe our granddaughter would really like it. Perhaps just wait until they come back from their games, and we can take them here to select. Their birthdays are coming soon after all!"

The seniors do not simply sit there and wait for the young ones. This is the non-apparent Left Circle, or "seemingly unrelated Left Circle", that theme parks may have missed. The character dolls and figurines that they sell provide the whole family with something in their homes to reminisce their happy time together. The seniors in the family want those to warm their hearts with memories. The needs can even be extended to the next generation when the young kids bring their own children to the theme park years later. The souvenirs that they brought back years ago set to remind them what they can now do for their children. While not yet born, the future children of the young kids then have become a "seemingly unrelated Left Circle" of the theme park.

Money Losing Telcos and App Developers

The next phenomenon probably cannot be explained well without using this very concept of "seemingly unrelated Left Circle". We often wonder how these smaller telecom companies (telcos) can sustain services with their very low prices. Their prices could be just half of what other telcos charge offering comparable signal quality. This is likely that smaller companies have to count on low prices to capture market shares. But ultimately we think they cannot run on a loss on every transaction that they make. What is their business model then?

What happens is that very often these smaller companies are bought up by larger companies a few years later. Why do those companies want to buy them? Obviously, it is for their customer base. When their customers are transferred to the larger companies, the latter can realize some economies of scale. What's more, there are opportunities to do cross selling with other products they already have as a bundle. Companies who take over smaller ones can also raise their profiles by a significant expansion in size. This will add a lot marketing power to them.

Now you find why in the last 3 years the small telco was selling below cost to gain customers. Its real Left Circle is not the day-to-day customers themselves. The Left Circle (the day-to-day customers) has in fact joined in as its Right Circle (the customer base). This makes it attractive for its real Left Circle, the invisible one, being the company who it believes will raise a takeover bid sooner or later.

Another puzzle we have is to figure out where all these free online apps can make money from. Almost all of us have experience in WhatsApp. We open free accounts in WhatsApp and are able to chat with friends and other people conveniently and efficiently without having to pay a cent. What does WhatsApp get by offering us all these services? What is its income source?

Of course, the example above has already given us some insight. We wonder how Facebook knows we are friends with someone and make recommendations for me to join up with her on Facebook? This is exactly the reason why Facebook wants to acquire WhatsApp. For all the data, naturally. When WhatsApp was first started, it concentrated on building its subscriber base. Once it has grown to a certain size, it is able to attract buyers such as Facebook. Facebook is interested not only in building up its scale but more importantly in acquiring the critical knowledge in subscriber-to-subscriber relationships through the data available in WhatsApp. Facebook gets substantial advantages through these additions.

Again, we may see WhatsApp's customers being its subscribers. But its income does not come from the users. It comes from the Left Circle that you cannot see — that is, Facebook who pays huge money to acquire it. Certainly, there are legality issues related to privacy and ownership of data, as well as whether users have given their consent for data transfer to Facebook. This is a matter that warrants some serious discussions. But for our purpose, we are not going to discuss them here.

Rewards from Public Services

We have many other examples of "seemingly unrelated Left Circle" around us. Perhaps one we find interesting is, why do top executives of companies, supposedly extremely busy, have time to perform community services? Those services range from being consultants for the government, or taking up Chairman or Vice Chairman positions in public organizations and NGOs, all without any monetary compensations. Sometimes, they even have to refrain from taking certain business opportunities to avoid possible conflicts of interest. Why are they doing this? Of course, there are various motives, including status and publicity, or relationship building with the government and important powers, or simply pure altruism aimed at delivering social good.

One message is clear from these appointments: the appointee has talent. When you are appointed by the government to give them advice, the government is your Left Circle, and your duty is to help them solve their problems. But as you are doing your job, you get known by a lot of people who keep an eye on your workstyle, expertise, level of intelligence and attitude. Those you come across are very important people, and the relationships you build will be extremely helpful in your career and future endeavours.

The persons you meet every day in the meeting room turn out to be your "non-apparent Left Circle". People offering their services may not have such an expectation when they first start, but very soon they will find that this setup embodies a lot of opportunities. As you perform your duty, you continue to develop credentials and accumulate credibility, making you a place to go to for expert advice. However, if conversely you demonstrate that you are tardy and limited, or even worse, you tend to take advantage of your position to gain personal benefits, then your reputation will go down as rapidly as you can imagine.

As you do your job the way it should be, genuinely wanting to work for the job purpose without treating it as one that carries a payback for you, you will develop your good name and reputation as an upright person. By offering your best to the job, somehow you will be rewarded handsomely at the end, even though you do not aim for it. This is not the kind of understanding that can be attained by using a simple Left Circle model. To do public services well, you simply do it for the best interest of the public.

To sum up, what we have to do is to be earnest and sincere, and to help others with our whole heart. A person doing this certainly is one that has sublime personality, giving others, whether old or young, rich or poor, friends or not, their due respect. All these virtues will bring back pertinent rewards, intrinsic and more. All this is to say, when you want to do good deeds, just do it whole-heartedly without caring about rewards. Your integrity and sincerity, while not intended for show, will be noticed by others. Very likely, people that you do not even know will see you as someone they can trust to offer you very good opportunities.

Here is another personal example of the professor. He has brought together someone who wanted a good staff and someone who wanted a good job. He has not thought of a reward in any form such as a commission. But the satisfied boss thinks, "How good is this professor! I might want to see if I have any staff who I can send to his EMBA course for development." The staff coming to the professor's EMBA course are his Left Circle, but they are not the people he has known or been in touch with. This is his "seemingly unrelated Left Circle". He gets this Left Circle because he is just doing a job, an unrelated job, in a way he thinks right for him.

People would ask: Why do we want to do good deeds? Those who ask this question may have a very shallow understanding of the world. Things happening in this world are a lot more complex than a simple relationship of getting paid for things you do. You do not do things only for getting paid. If you hold this concept of wanting to get paid every time, you may end up losing many of your "seemingly unrelated Left Circles". You shut the door for them.

Once a youngster went to his girlfriend's home and met a lady who wanted to enter the building as well. He politely opened the door for her. Soon he found that the lady was his future mother-in-law. Of course, when he opened the door for the lady, he had no idea she was his girlfriend's mother. If he had ever thought of this possibility, he might have overacted. He just happened to be a modest person who would do the same for anyone. By doing so, he must have made a lot of positive impressions on a lot of seemingly unrelated persons. This seemingly unrelated act by him leads to a happy ending: His girlfriend was happy to marry him and they live happily ever after.

EMBA Public Broadcast Programmes

The last but not least, we have another example about CUHK EMBA. Many people wonder why our CUHK EMBA programme would produce 44 episodes of "New Thinking in Management" and 8 episodes of "Talking to CEOs" to be broadcast on the radio every year. What do we want to get from the broadcast?

Thinking back, it was the radio people who proposed that we produce a programme of this nature to enable the public to obtain a better understanding of management and strategic issues, so as to improve people's general ability at work. At that time, we had no motive for any benefit to our EMBA programme and simply believed it was a good thing for society. As we organized this for the public, we called up quite a few friends, and all of them agreed it was a very good idea. Since the start, many CEOs of big corporations and talented people have gladly accepted our invitation to come to our radio programme as guests.

About five to seven years ago, we started to spot some interesting developments. When we asked the EMBA applicants why they wanted to join the programme, some said they had listened to our radio programmes for 5 years. Some even said, "My boss asks me to come here. He has listened to your programme for 10 years. He said if a programme can uphold the same principles for 10 years, it must be highly trustable. After all, nobody can repeat the same lies for 10 years. There should be a group of excellent teaching staff running this programme, and we definitely want to get associated." We had not met this boss, nor did we know who he was and where he came from. But he was giving back to us for what we did for the public.

While we are doing things out of goodwill, our result is that we get some "seemingly unrelated Left Circles". Some of these unintended Left Circles turn out to be our Left Circles, making themselves students of ours, while others exert influence on our other Left Circles and create positive public opinions. As they advocate the idea of "honest business", we are grateful that they have offered help, giving our education sector a big boost in spreading our belief.

We have always been advocating the use of conscience in business. Whether we want to be innovative or just be steadily competent in business, we are working towards public good. We support staff's livelihoods and use our management skills to help build a better society. This is the process that turns "seemingly unrelated Left Circles" into our "Left Circles of Left Circle". It requires consistency and persistence to get good results. If we had run our radio programmes only for 5 years, we would not have yielded the same result that we have today.

Beneficiaries of our radio programmes are not only the teachers and prospective students. The existing students are very much motivated and encouraged too. At times we ask our students to host the show, while at other times they just come as audiences. Their presence in the programme reinforces their learning in class. We do not want our students to just come and make the event a full house. We want them to come as key players. The students are both our Left Circle and our Right Circle in this endeavour.

Those coming to the show include the current students, former students, friends and others who are interested in making contributions. We are giving these people a platform to share and exchange, hoping that they can be a part of the effort to cultivate a higher ethos for the society. We also hope that our sharing of the business wisdom behind management, strategic planning and leadership can guide positive general behaviours. Our EMBA programme certainly has these as our targets. But we did not plan to have these same targets for our radio programmes. Those scenarios that emerge only make us realize that these can be our possible objectives. The development that we have seen through our radio programmes can only be explained using this "seemingly unrelated Left Circle" concept.

As we speak, you may start to realize that we are indeed talking about potentially everybody to be our "seemingly unrelated Left Circle". As long as we do not care what the result is, putting our best in everything that we do and using our heart and soul to help others as much as possible, we can potentially turn any "seemingly unrelated Left Circle" to become our Right Circle.

This chapter tells us that if you use a short-sighted approach to pursue immediate benefits, making efforts only to get deals done with the most obvious Left Circles, we would not go very far. There are numerous ways to run our business. If we can integrate all the approaches given in our chapters here, we can form a very nice picture of what it takes to get ourselves up to run a superb business.

Chapter 10

Summing Up Left-Right Circles with Four Axioms

Coming to the last chapter, we wish to sum up using four axioms that combine to become our motto. The axioms make it easy for us to grasp the strategic considerations behind our Left-Right Circles theory. These four axioms are:

(1) Build upon the past and develop the future — striving to do good work.
(2) Take the Left Circle as your guide — with boundless innovation and enhancement.
(3) Match the Left and Right Circles — enjoying perfect harmony in what you do.
(4) Wallow not in your present success — always looking ahead to the next step.

Build Upon the Past and Develop the Future — Striving To Do Good Work

Let us look at what it means by "build upon the past and develop the future — striving to do good work". When we contemplate strategies or solutions to our issues, we normally use reference points — that is, things that happened in the past as background.

We usually look at these issues: Which customer groups did we serve? What skills or competences did we use to make them our customers? How did they get hooked to go through the process of "know it, understand it, like it, do it, and get used to it"? How did they get to "know it"? Through what channels and by what communications did we get them to "understand it"? In what features did they start to "like it"? What linked them and us together? After they liked us, how did they "do it" with purchases? What can we take as future references? Did they "get used of it" to become their habit after purchasing the product? Did they help to build word-of-mouth for us? Did they become the models for others to follow? Did they come back or just forget about us?

To build upon the past and develop the future, we need to take reference from "the past" before developing ideas for "the future" The important point here is that we have to understand what contributed to the past events so as to inspire us to find our way into the future.

Why is an understanding of the past so important in running business? Take this example: If you come to a new job, the worst thing you can possibly do is to immediately replace the system there by the one you have been using. Some may think, "What I have been doing is working, so why can't it work here?" What they have missed is that the two companies are different with different environments, so they have very different "pasts". They also have different reputations and advantages especially considering the people that are there.

What are the characteristics and aspirations of the staff? Do they have any dreams over and above the salary? You may have had very good staff before who worked extra hard. But in a new company, without knowing the whole background including the culture, operating model, financial and resource strength, and general norm, you are at risk of upsetting a lot of things if you do not apply the principles of "building on the past to develop the future".

One set of strategies does not apply in all situations. Before you decide on your specific direction, you have to understand the company's Left Circle, how the Area C is formed, and where this Area C is likely to move. Only when you are crystal clear about all these characteristics will you be able to get your management work done well as you venture into the future.

From the past moving on to the future, what we strive is to do good work. This is the ultimate aim of the Left-Right Circles theory. Without achieving good work, the business may only be operating on a form rather than substance. How did the culture of this company come about? What pushes staff morale high in this company? For what do people trust this company? This is closely related to the good work that we have done.

What is "good work"? It is beyond what Marketing 1.0 prescribes. Work under Marketing 1.0 is to complete sales. But "good work" is not only about producing benefits for the company. When you sell your product, would the customers find it good because it can satisfy their needs? For Marketing 2.0, you have to make customers willing to buy your product, because it is the product that satisfies their needs. Is that "good work" already? We think it is not enough. We believe it has to go to at least Marketing 3.0. Our business has to make the whole system work better, with everyone benefiting through improved life quality or lower price level.

The system we refer to here is not restricted to the customers. When customers are genuinely willing to buy your product, are your own people also happy about it? If your staff are not happy, is it "good work"? Now that your staff are happy, are your investors also happy? Are your suppliers happy? Is the whole society happy and feeling grateful that your business is there? Is your business wasting valuable natural resources or polluting the environment leaving harmful effects for future generations? There are multiple aspects that you need to consider, which determines if you are really doing "good work".

Should you run your business for the purpose making maximum profit? Certainly, profit is necessary for you to sustain. Should your company collapse, your staff and society at large will suffer. But businesses should not take profit as the sole purpose. First of all, are you happy doing the things you do every day? Are you bringing joy or agony to your staff the way you run your business? What has your company brought to the community?

The best scenario is that you are helping people with the work you do and others are happy because you are here, and your staff feel secure and motivated under your leadership. However, if your family and friends are not willing to talk about you, then you must not be doing "good work", even though you bring money back for your family and loved ones.

What kind of inspiration do we find in our first axiom? It is to prompt us to use other people's angles to look back at us, other people being our various Left Circles. Their inter-relationships create a lot of angles and demands. How can we achieve a balance from all those demands and angles? We know any decisions we make will not be able to please everyone. Sometimes we notice even what some people ask for may not be for their own best interest. We need to understand the whole scenario and the entire background in order to find that balance. This is the best way to move everybody forward.

What do we want to achieve from "building on the past to develop the future"? It is to "strive to do good work", targeting results that deliver benefits to as many people as we wish. The result that we wish to achieve is not too different from what is called a "great harmony". Now having our concepts, we have to find our steps to make it happen. We wish to create benefits that can go as widely as possible for the community. This describes our first objective.

Take the Left Circle as Your Guide — With Boundless Innovation and Enhancement

How do we make the first axiom happen? The aspiration behind the Left-Right Circles theory is "aspiring to do good work", but the guiding principle is "taking the Left Circle as the guide". The starting point of the whole thinking process is the recipient targets. We should ask, "What are their needs?" Our targets can usually describe their needs. At times, they cannot. But even when they cannot specify, we have to estimate what needs they have.

Going a step further, there are needs that our targets have but do not recognize they have. For example, when you ask a small child what he wants to do, he will tell you all things that do not help, such as keeping on playing. It does not mean it is not good for the child to play games, but he has no idea what other useful things, such as learning, group activities and service to others, can do for him. So, do you expect your targets to tell you all their needs? Taking the Left Circle as your guide, you can dig deep into what good work means.

Apart from the obvious targets, we should be mindful of the "seemingly unrelated Left Circle". We want to activate those non-apparent needs that we discussed in Chapter 8. The Left-Right Circles theory is not simple. The person who comes to buy your product may not be the one who decides what product to buy. Also, the one who decides to buy your product may not be the one who uses it.

In your school, you see an office assistant coming to collect an application form. He is sent by the parents who are the decision-makers for their child to come here to study. If you are the school principal, who do you think are in your Left Circle? Obviously, all of them. You can rather easily understand the relationship between the parents and the child, but you need also to realize how important the assistant can be. If he fails to collect the form, the whole transaction fails. When the assistant asks about the application form, do you ask him to download from the web or come in person? If he comes, how would you treat him?

If you think along this line, you are Left Circle guided. As the school principal, you cannot just focus on trying to please the person who pays. The consideration has to be broad. You have to be careful about the possible caveats if you ignore certain members in your Left Circle.

When you practise using the Left Circle as a guide, you should not forget your Internal Left Circle. In Chapter 4, you have read that a lot of things are not possible without the Internal Left Circle. What does the Internal Left Circle want? Only getting paid? Of course, they need to be paid. You will face serious problems if you do not do the very basic. But can pay alone give them the drive to do excellent work? No. They are concerned if the job has future, if they are happy doing it, and if they have good friends and colleagues working with them, just to mention a few.

Care from the boss is also important. As some staff grow older, would they be given jobs that utilize their experience more than other aspects that they find difficulties coping with? Would they need to make too much adjustment? Is there enough support? Do they have the applicable tools? Overall, would the working environment be favourable to everyone? Not that it needs to be a lavish setting, but a friendly environment with helpful colleagues is important. The company's image has an effect on its Internal Left Circle too. These are just some of the issues concerning the Internal Left Circle. It shows it is easy to say we are Left Circle guided but it is not as easy to take on board all that is required.

Other than needs, you have to keep tabs on the behaviours of your Left Circle. Where can you get them to know you? To certain people, you may have the best product in the world, but they simply have not heard about you. Why? Probably you do not know how to connect with them. How do people obtain information? Is it by pull or by push? If you have a firm grasp of this valuable information, you may devise methods that can subtly let your presence be felt before they notice it. You cannot be Left Circle guided if you do not even know the behaviours of your Left Circle. Which media are the best for you to get to your Left Circle? What message is appropriate? What do you do that gives you the best chance of getting them to like you? These are important considerations surrounding the Left Circle.

To be Left Circle guided, the issues you have to look into when you do selling and buying are prices, product features, logistics and selling locations, etc. Does advertising and promotion have a role in this? Are you thinking that you can totally avoid expensive advertising when your excellent product can do the trick? But if without broad communication, how can customers know you have this product? That would affect selling, of course. And if you do not sell well, the company will suffer.

Going a step further, after your Left Circle bought your product, what do the buyers think? How different is their view of your product compared with that before buying? Normally there is some difference, at least in terms of how they understand it. But would they buy it again? Comparing products that have 80% and 20% rebuying interest, you can see the differences in terms of the reactions of the Left Circle. You need those critical insights.

What we have to also pay attention to is, after you have satisfied your Left Circle, their needs may start changing. When your Left Circle starts to move left, part of your Area C (the overlap area between the Left and Right Circles) may soon become an Area E (the part in your Area C that has fallen out of the Left Circle as the latter moves), by which time the Left Circle you used to have is no longer your Left Circle. Why do they leave? How would a new Area D (the enlarged overlap area into the Left Circle when the Right Circle moves left) come in? How do you get new customers? You can review the Left-Right Circles concept in Figure 1.

Even when you are Left Circle guided, you do not have to satisfy everyone in the market. You have to choose your targets. In doing so, you take risks. There is always a chance that you have chosen a target that you should not have, or have not chosen a target that you should have, or have not given up a target that you should have.

As we can see, there are many issues to look after to be Left Circle guided. But some people do not even follow this approach. Some people are simply "Right Circle guided". They put themselves at the centre of the universe, pushing what they have out to the world. They do not think too much about whether those things can serve other people's needs. They cannot conduct meaning communications with their customers or prospects. Many research results tell us that the best way to communicate is to listen first. Listening is to understand your Left Circle, which in essence, is the very important first act of being Left Circle guided.

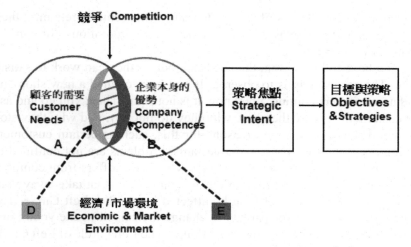

Figure 1: Reviewing Area D and Area E of Left-Right circles.

The things that ought to happen guided by the Left Circle are "different levels of innovation and enhancement". How far you can go depends on how deep your understanding is and how deep you can use your thinking mind. But if you do not let your Left Circle guide you and prefer to stand still, you will surely be overtaken by your hard-thinking and hard-working competitors. They will do what you do not. What fight is it between you and your competitors? It is how deep you can dig into your innovative mind following what your Left Circle tells you.

There are several levels of needs from customers: (1) their current needs, (2) needs they cannot describe clearly, and (3) needs they have not even thought about. If you cannot go deep, you have limited ability to compete effectively in the market. Beyond that, you also have to attract new customers to become your new Left Circles. All these call for different levels of innovation and enhancement that you have to draw from your Left Circle understanding.

Take the banks as an example. The banks started with mainly helping people to save. Then, their services extended to trade finance, followed by mutual trusts and insurance products that they sell with other financial institutions. Today, you can find a wide array of joint financial products available from the banks. From the bank's initial point of view, these are breakthrough innovations. Banks today are not the same banks you saw in those days. Should they be Right Circle focused, they would not have made this happen. Using the Left Circle as their guide, the banks manage to roll out various levels of innovation and enhancement, retaining their position as a crucial player for consumers and corporations alike in the financial world.

You have to know what the needs are before they can work to satisfy them. The easiest way is to observe. If you have opened a new shop and find no customers coming, you know it is not right. Then, you go and ask the customers — why they buy, why they do not buy, and why they stop buying. There can be many reasons for this, such as certain customers having been upset by your shop assistants. Problems are not confined to the product. Customers can be lured away by better offers from competitors. It may also be better promotions by competitors that take away your customers. Your Left Circle can be affected by another Left Circle. The son may be the cause for parents to change their habit as the young one wants new things instead of the same things. The Left Circle of Left Circle has a lot of influence.

As more media and techniques are available, you have more ways to learn about your customers. From surveys to focus groups, you find increasingly better techniques to gauge customer needs. Customer Relationship Management (CRM) system, data mining and Big Data are the latest inventions that can be extremely useful. Again, endless innovative methods are coming out on all levels.

When customers buy certain products, what are the related products they also want to buy? What are their motives in buying? Sometimes even the buyers themselves are not too sure about their own motives. Big Data analytics today can deduce these motives by linking up their buying decisions and behaviours. When you go to an online bookstore, you are greeted first with book recommendations. As data about your past activities are stored there, the store can deduce your preferences and make relevant recommendations. As you are introduced to new books tracing back to your interests, there is every chance that you will buy.

Finding the key link is very important. When you identify the link between two products, you can package them together to sell. When someone opens a bank account and deposit some money, you immediately see an opportunity. Using the advanced systems we talk about or simply your keen eye, some valuable insights can surface. When you notice your customer is buying insurance for his domestic helper, you can sense there is a change in the family condition. Could it that they are expecting a new baby? Would they have a need for an education fund or related insurance product? Using this approach, you deepen your thinking process and search for solutions. This is the approach you may use to bring continuous innovation and enhancement.

How deep and broad our thinking goes has big effects on the wider social progress. This drive for understanding broadens our knowledge base and inspires new ways of doing things. Very often, it creates a wow factor with people exclaiming, "Wow, how can you think of this?" If you do that, you will be successful.

The world keeps changing, and likewise the market is changing too. The changes around your Left Circle will move them on. The Left Circle is constantly looking for better and less costly offerings. They are expecting higher efficiency and better service quality from you. Even if they are not as specific and aggressive, eventually other forces such as their own Left Circles, the general environment and the competitive environment will move them on. This tells you that if you choose to stand still and not use your Left Circle to guide you moving forward, you will be left behind by others.

Match the Left and Right Circles — Enjoying Perfect Harmony in What You Do

The first axiom stipulates that we have to use our background and the strengths it provides to do good work. The second axiom gives the direction for doing good work, which is to deliver more and better benefits to the Left Circle in response to their needs. Understanding clearly the different levels of needs, we can provide very innovative and high-quality solutions.

The two axioms do not form the whole picture. As you understand what the Left Circle needs, the question then is whether your Right Circle is able to deliver the solutions. While you show you can do it today, there is danger that your Right Circle may not be able to keep up with changes in the Left Circle as time goes by. People keep having more demanding needs and higher expectations. Particularly as technology brings new solutions, your competitors may harness technology better and do things that you cannot do. A lot of time, it is not that you do not know what is needed, only that you have problems delivering. How capable are you? How strong is your Right Circle? You need to keep your Right Circle strong to have a place in the market.

Of course, it is not as simple as just having the technology. Although technology is important, ultimately it is your capability that makes you better in delivering satisfying solutions for the Left Circle. Technology is there to help but not to determine. "Matching the Left and Right Circles" is to have the Left Circle needs in firm grasp, and then match up those needs using your Right Circle competences. Matching up is the whole point of our Left-Right Circles theory.

Matching up does not mean that you just have a "best" product to help you satisfy all your customers. Oftentimes, the best quality product is not what the Left Circle needs. The product with the best quality often is the most expensive, but the Left Circle may not need that level of quality for the sake of the price. The best is therefore not the best quality per se, but the best in terms of the match-up.

We have mentioned that sometimes the Left Circle may not know what they want, and we have to estimate their needs to provide a product or offering that appeals to them. The wonder in all this is that we can predict their needs and get ourselves ahead of time to prepare for the product. The lead time for a product can be as long as a few years. Of course, taking such an approach involves risks, but if you are confident about the Left Circle needs as well as your own Right Circle capability, you get the advantage of an early head start. Chances are you become superior to your competitors in this race.

"Being superior" is not measured by profit, nor by a high ranking. It has to be measured by whether you are doing "good work". What "good work" have you done to this world so the recipients of your good work feel happy because you are here? Will they feel sad if without you? If you have stopped selling your product, will they feel sad about it? If they do miss you, you prove yourself to have great value to them. Yet there are still times when you have to stop selling a certain product because it has not captured enough sales. There are still people loving it. It is quite likely that your competitors have just produced something that more people like.

Can you serve your Left Circle needs with a nice balance of price and quality in your product? It is not easy, but it is a measure of how you perform in matching up your Left and Right Circles. Timing is another factor. You catch the right timing now, but very soon it will come and pass because the market is moving on and looking for other things. In that case, you have to adjust.

We are living in a dynamic world where nothing is a given. You need to make the right decisions in this changing environment. You have to look at the megatrends and the big picture to ascertain forward movements and developments that you have to make. It is important that you pay enough attention to understanding people, including your Left Circle, your Internal Left Circle, your competitors, and other related Left Circles such the media, general public, activists and pressure groups. You need to find your position, hopefully a unique position. Once you have made your position clear, your various Left Circles will come and interpret what it means to them. As such, when you set your position, you have to assess how your various Left Circles will look at it, and gauge the consequences.

Once your position is clear, you follow it with your strategy or action plan. A good strategy is one that looks after all the needs of your Left Circle. As the best strategist, you can guide your Left Circle to appreciate that they deserve better choices, and then you lead them to the better choice you offer. The choice you provide completely matches their needs, whether those needs are specified, not specified, or even not imagined. The process is difficult to describe. The matching play between the Left and Right Circles is akin to a tango dance, or a beautiful football game where the players move in sync with perfect coordination, all the while without requiring any visible orders or commands. Intuitively, the players have perfect mutual understanding playing as a team.

How can you get your Left and Right Circles to play in a perfect harmony? Your strategy has to be inspired and led by this vision. If you see it enough for customers to just buy your product, then you are far from your ideal situation. The very least has to be that your customers feel happy after buying your product. But if people all around agree that your product is worth buying and help to propagate a positive message out to let more people know, then you are able to build upon that to further develop. Your business will continue to grow until you see "your Left and Right Circles are perfectly matched and live in a perfect harmony."

Now, we have reached that point that a perfect match between your Left and Right Circles exists and you are in a perfect harmony. But it does not mean it will remain the same in the next stage. You need to respond to change, preferably before it occurs. Change happens often when you least expect it. Your Left Circle can give you a hint, or change is prompted by new technology. The change can either put you back because you are unable to match a practice or propel you with another edge because you know how to utilize the technology. Your Right Circle will need to chase the Left Circle forever, because the Left Circle always moves left. If your

Right Circle fails to match up, your Area C will eventually become redundant. Your market share will shrink and your business will face a hard time against the market forces.

To maintain harmony and have the capability to react quickly to change, you have to constantly observe if balance is maintained between the Left and Right Circles. As one side changes, the other side needs corresponding change. You need to stay at the forefront of technology, and have yourself ready for change once it is required. You need to keep a firm grasp of how the change affects your Left Circle, Left Circle of Left Circle and seemingly unrelated Left Circle. Technology will tilt your Left-Right Circles balance, but nobody can tell you exactly how and when this will happen. What you can count on is to follow the principles embodied in our axioms to strive for this perfect balance and harmony.

An important job of yours is to move Right Circle left to find your Area D. No one can give you a formula for this, since it is a "blue ocean" (newly developed market) where no one has been before. This blue ocean is constructed through change that occurs and the right moves that you make every day. It occurs amidst all the changes in the general environment and in the competition. These changes happen one after another.

Should you find competitors encroaching on you, how should you respond? A head-on fight may not be the best way. You may follow the principle of doing "good work" to find the best spot to establish your position. But if your competitors are also finding their spots to do "good work", will there be conflicts? Different types of "good work" can be done by different people, due to their different backgrounds, cultures, abilities and supporting resources. These differences take us to do things in different ways. Our cups of tea are different, and we have different objects to shoot. One size cannot fit all.

We have given you all the dimensions that are needed for creating "perfect harmony". When you push forward, you cannot drive your way through mindlessly. Your momentum comes from a fine balance that you maintain. When you lose your momentum, it will be difficult to catch back up. Other people will find new territories that will be unreachable to you. Masters of the game nurture their fighting abilities through practices in battle, continuously sharpening their strategic skills. Your skills cannot be nurtured behind closed doors. Superb skills cannot be created in a vacuum. You need to be in the game to win it.

Wallow Not in Your Present Success — Always Looking Ahead to the Next Step

The fourth axiom is "wallowing not in your present success but always looking ahead to the next step". This axiom can be considered the mother of the first axiom which is "building on the past to develop the future and always striving to do good work." You ought to ask yourself this question every day: What is the next step? While you are doing very well today, establishing your Area C with very happy customers, what are you going to do beyond the current success? The obvious answer is finding your new Area D.

Area D is a new territory and new direction. It counts on your Right Circle power to push through into new areas that will address needs yet to be satisfied. The Right Circle is not yet there, but those unserved needs are indeed very close to what you can do, so your Right Circle will develop new capabilities that will take you into this new Area D.

Why do you want to push through beyond your current success? It is because by your ability to do good work built on your present and past, you can carry this power on to the next step. Where will the next step end? As you know, the Left Circle never stops moving, and you have to continuously go forward to match it. What do you wish to achieve in going beyond our current success? You hope to use your Right Circle to serve your customers better, achieving a perfect match-up between the Left and Right Circles to enjoy a perfect harmony.

Among all the competitors, why are you considered the most suitable one to go for this? It is because you have the insights and innovative ideas. Not all technologies will gain immediate acceptance, which means you have to make adaptations. The key is in finding out how these technologies can be applied to satisfy the needs. New technologies may not appear to suit the current needs, but you can think of the needs of the Left Circle of Left Circle, the seemingly unrelated Left Circle, as well as the unrecognized needs of your Left Circle, which may have applications. Those are the directions that you can follow to go beyond your current success.

When you decide that you should "go beyond your current success", we "look ahead to the next step". This is to remind us that there is always a better tomorrow. Room for improvement is unlimited. To quote the *I-Ching*: "The sky is the limit for people who want to self-improve," This prompts us to consistently improve our Right Circle and seek a new Area

D. As experimenting turns the whole environment into a new normal, we can make this process into a regular one for constant renewal. We replace the old ways with this new normal to stay in the game. Whether the "new setting" belongs to us or others, it will depend on how strong and innovative we can be. Strength is not measured in financial terms. It is more in whether we can develop our capability as a strong team and focus our effort on satisfying our Left Circle. Our effort towards the Left Circle ought to be relentless, producing results that our Left Circle did not expect.

To advance to the next step, we need a fresh new process. What is the requirement to be a professor? The old requirement was that a professor teaches in the classroom. What is the new requirement? It is that he teaches something practicable, and not purely "academic". What more is expected? The professor is now also expected to develop friendly relationships with the students, and be willing to explore new ways of doing things with an open mind.

Are there any more requirements? Of course, there are. How good is his external networking? Apart from being good friends with the students, he has to have good links with outside. He has to be good in theories and practices, helping students to step out to the world. He has to help students develop kindness, righteousness, propriety, wisdom and trust to solve world problems. The key is not in how clever and knowledgeable the professor is. It is in whether he can make the students more intelligent and more capable to make contributions to the world. To make it happen, the professor has to go beyond his current success and look ahead to the next step. If he does not do that himself, he can hardly expect his students to do the same.

The next step also has to have a social purpose. The professor we just talked about will have to deliver contributions socially on top of teaching in class. To transfer this logic back into the business context, a company has to have positive influences on the wider community.

No matter what organization or profession you are in, whether you are a professor, architect, manager, librarian, prison officer or any government official, there is always a need to look ahead to as the next step. Otherwise, you will be left behind failing even to fulfil your current duty. How can you go the next step and reset your context? It has to be doing good work. It has to be guided by the Left Circle. It has to be with boundless innovation and enhancement. It has to be a perfect harmony between the Left and Right Circles. It never stops. Once you have done all these, you are set to go on to another next step.

When the new setting is established, your situation today will be the reference you use as your past that helps you define your next move. The cycle repeats, and you will back there to start again: "to build on your past to develop your future". The fourth axiom ends as the first axiom starts again. You continue to delve deep into this concept, and more and more you realize these are principles for business as well as for personal development. The Left-Right Circles theory applies not only in business settings but also in personal, family, government, interpersonal, NGO and social enterprise settings.

Index

Printed in the United States
by Baker & Taylor Publisher Services